THE ESSENTIAL ART OF WAR

SUN-TZU PING-FA

THE
ESSENTIAL
ART
OF
WAR

*Translated, with Historical Introduction
and Commentaries, by* Ralph D. Sawyer
with the collaboration of Mei-chün Lee Sawyer

BASIC
B A Member of the Perseus Books Group
New York
BOOKS

Published by Basic Books,
A Member of the Perseus Books Group

Books published by Basic Books are available at special discounts for
bulk purchases in the United States by corporations, institutions, and
other organizations. For more information, please contact the Special
Markets Department at the Perseus Books Group, 11 Cambridge
Center, Cambridge, MA 02142, or special.markets@perseusbooks.com.

Designed by Trish Wilkinson
Set in 11.5-pt Goudy by the Perseus Books Group

Library of Congress Cataloging-in-Publication Data

Sunzi, 6th cent. B.C.
    [Sunzi bing fa. English]
    The essential art of war — Sun-tzu ping-fa / translated, with
historical introduction and commentaries, by Ralph D. Sawyer ; with
the collaboration of Mei-chün Lee Sawyer.
        p.   cm.
    Includes index.
    ISBN-13: 978-0-465-07204-0 (hardcover) 1. Military art and
science — Early works to 1800. I. Title: Sun-tzu ping-fa. II. Sawyer,
Ralph D. III. Sawyer, Mei-chün. IV. Title.

U101.S9513 2005
355.02—dc22   2005013769
ISBN 0-465-07204-6

05   06   07   08   /   10   9   8   7   6   5   4   3   2   1

Contents

Preface

The intent of *The Essential Art of War* is to provide a comprehensive yet succinct introduction to Sun-tzu's remarkable and often enigmatic *Art of War*. Thus, apart from entailing a somewhat different orientation and encompassing significant new materials, it differs from our well-known, single-volume *Art of War* and the translation embodied in our *Seven Military Classics* by excising material of interest primarily to scholars; drastically condensing the historical background; deleting the lengthy tactical analysis of the era's pivotal battles; and selectively discussing the core concepts.

The core text has been based upon the heavily annotated, traditional Sung dynasty edition not only because it reflects the understanding of the past fifteen hundred years, the beliefs upon which government and military officials based their actions, but also because it continues to be widely circulated throughout Asia.

Although the translation has been adopted from our *Art of War*, individual sentences and certain important passages have been succinctly expanded with crucial tomb text materials that resolve otherwise opaque passages, supplement obvious deficiencies, or add new insights; some passages have also been slightly reshaped and occasionally rephrased to make them more accessible upon first reading, though without ever simplifying the terminology or "dumbing down" the text.

Explanatory material will be found not only in the newly written introduction but also in an afterword and the few paragraphs appended to each chapter. Apart from setting the basic historical constraints and reprising Sun-tzu's infamous biography, the introduction examines the nature of the text and the implications for the reader. The chapter commentaries then identify the core concepts and place some of the less obvious elements in context by elucidating key aspects and demystifying their organic relationships. Finally, the afterword discusses crucial issues that merit more extended treatment by broadening the interpretation within Sun-tzu's essential vision and suggesting some contemporary resonances. Although the book's internal logic and occasional opacity significantly delimit the range and choice of topics, questions raised in numerous corporate, military, and intelligence seminars over the past three decades, as well as queries to our

Web site (www.ralphsawyer.com), have considerably shaped their treatment.

With the aid of these introductory materials readers should have no difficulty in envisioning and selectively adopting Sun-tzu's principles and concepts to life or business situations. Because the *Art of War*'s passages were the product of military activities realized by men and forces in the turmoil of command and tumult of battle, their initial or primary understanding should be martial. Only thereafter can they be successfully extrapolated and mapped onto other domains of endeavor. To this end, the afterword offers a few suggestions for a broader applicability and an overview of the darker implications; but as with the chapter comments, they are provided as a matter of explication. *Determining the utility, legality, and appropriateness, if any, to individual situations and activities of all the materials included in the* Essential Art of War *remains the reader's responsibility.*

Although our concise book is thus intended to be read as a fully independent work, it can also be used in conjunction with our single-volume *Art of War*, which contains a lengthy examination of Sun-tzu's life and the book's authorship, an extensive historical introduction featuring the key battles of his era, a systematic analysis of the main concepts, additional tomb writings and other materials, and numerous textual and historical notes. Further understanding may also be gleaned from some of the other writings discussed in the brief section for suggested reading and from the comments to our other Sun-tzu volume, *The Complete Art of War*.

Ralph Sawyer
Summer, 2005

A Note on Pronunciation

Unfortunately, neither of the two commonly employed orthographies makes the pronunciation of Romanized Chinese characters easy. Each system has its stumbling blocks and we remain unconvinced that *qi* in *pinyin* is inherently more comprehensible to unpracticed readers than the older, increasingly discarded Wade-Giles *ch'i*, although it is certainly no less comprehensible than *j* for *r* in Wade-Giles. However, because many of the important terms may already be familiar, a number of previous *Art of War* translations as well as all our martial writings employ Wade-Giles; and as a minor protest against the political practices of the PRC's draconian regime, we continue to employ it here. Nevertheless, for the convenience of younger readers, key romanizations in *pinyin* have also been provided in parentheses, although well-known cities, names, and books are retained in their customary forms.

As a crude guide to pronunciation, we offer the following notes on the significant exceptions to normally expected sounds:

t, as in *Tao*: without apostrophe, pronounced as a *d* (*pinyin* "*d*")

p, as in *ping*: without apostrophe, pronounced as a *b* (*pinyin* "*b*")

ch, as in *chuang*: without apostrophe, pronounced as a *j* (*pinyin* "*j*" *and* "*zh*")

hs, as in *hsi*: pronounced *she* (*pinyin* "*x*")

j, as in *jen*: pronounced as an *r* (*pinyin* "*r*")

Thus, the name of the famous Chou (or Zhou in *pinyin*) dynasty is pronounced as if written "jou" and sounds just like the English name "Joe."

Dynastic Chronology

Legendary Sage Emperors	2852–2255 B.C.E.
Hsia (Xia)	2205–1766
Shang	1766–1045
Chou (Zhou)	
Western Chou (Zhou)	1045–770
Eastern Chou (Zhou)	770–256
Spring and Autumn	722–481
Warring States	403–221
Ch'in (Qin)	221–207
Former Han (Western Han)	206–008 C.E.
Later Han (Eastern Han)	023–220
Six Dynasties	222–589
Three Kingdoms	168–280
Sui	589–618
T'ang (Tang)	618–907
Five Dynasties	907–959
Sung	960–1126

Southern Sung	1127–1279
Yüan (Mongol)	1279–1368
Ming	1368–1644
Ch'ing (Manchu) (Qing)	1644–1911

Introduction

Spawned during a period of increasingly horrific and incessant military strife, Sun-tzu's *Ping-fa*, or *Art of War*, quickly became the progenitor for a continuous, literate tradition of military science. Doubtlessly the most important book in China's long and vaunted history apart from the Confucian *Analects*, it disproportionately influenced the conceptions, actions, and lives of untold millions over the centuries of interminable strife and frequent fragmentation that marred the state's tenuous geopolitical unity. Studied and adopted by strategists and commanders, its tactical principles repeatedly determined the fate of armies, life and death of the state, and very existence or extinction of vast segments of the populace.

Even more remarkable, rather than having vanished and become forgotten, the *Art of War*'s impact not only continues undiminished, but continues to expand and penetrate every conceivable realm of human endeavor. Its renewed vitality is visible not just in the martial sphere, where the worldwide revolution in military affairs has prompted the People's Republic of China (PRC) to reexamine its concepts and principles as an integral part of their ongoing search for a new military doctrine with unique Chinese characteristics, but also in the domains of business, personal relations, social interaction, the stock market, and the minutiae of everyday life. However, it's not the enigmatic, often opaque classical text that is read and pondered, but an astounding variety of contemporary modern-language versions.

These vernacular versions range from highly simplified, plain language translations through every imaginable variation and peregrination, including lavish illustrated editions and classical texts complete with traditional but expansive commentaries that explore not just the immediate meaning but also extended implications and connotations, some wildly divergent, others simply the product of the writer's imagination. Numerous colorful comic-book versions have also appeared, some cheap, pithy productions printed on execrable paper that yet sell hundreds of thousands, others finely detailed multivolume episodic tales intended primarily for Sun-tzu afficionados.

A variety of dedicated texts interpret the *Art of War* from a predetermined, systematized perspective such as Taoism or Buddhism; expand the "true implications" through personal, sometimes bizarre insights; or adopt the principles and concepts to one or another specialized realm, particularly general business practices such as marketing and organizational management. Especially interesting are programs intended for singles seeking to vanquish the opposite sex and works discussing how husbands and wives may control their marriage partners or even nurture exciting new loves outside of wedlock. Although some of these works are characterized by levity, most are deadly serious in intent and execution.

Passages from the *Art of War* also permeate popular culture and the contemporary media, frequently being cited or employed in movie subplots, serialized television dramas, and short stories and novels, whether or not they involve a martial theme. The principles and concepts are used almost daily in newspaper analyses of world events such as the Iraq conflict, generalized Middle Eastern and Islamic tensions, major business and economic developments, and all aspects of the competitive Asian environment where China's burgeoning power is viewed with increasing trepidation. Attesting to their ubiquitousness, many underpin academic analyses and detailed strategic assessments of the greater international geopolitical struggle.

Sun-tzu's thinking similarly pervades Japanese and, to a lesser extent, Korean and Singaporean popular culture; and for centuries the *Art of War* has heavily impacted traditional military practices and science in

Vietnam, Japan, and Korea. This phenomenon has not been confined to Asia but is similarly witnessed in the West, where translations of the *Art of War* have not only been available for two centuries but also continue to multiply in virtually every known format. Numerous variations and focal volumes explore the principles and their applicability in such realms as business and sports, and even U.S. military components have studied and consciously adopted many of the concepts and operational principles in increasingly shifting to maneuver warfare doctrine over the past three decades. Nor has exposure in the mass media lagged; movies such as *Wall Street*, the *Art of War*, and *Rising Sun* have all exploited the text for context and subplots. *The Sopranos* and even *The Simpsons* have occasionally quoted the *Art of War*, television's broad impact immediately creating a temporary surge in its popularity.

Apart from underpinning the Chinese mindset and strategic culture, numerous phrases from the *Art of War* have thus become well known and, much as American football coaches might claim that "the best defense is a good offense," have entered the language itself as popular sayings. Perhaps a reflection of China's abiding confidence in the ability of strategy and planning, deceit and manipulation, to allow inferior forces to overcome significantly stronger foes, these *ch'eng-yü (chengyu)* embody tactical fundamentals. Among the dozens commonly heard, the following are particularly prominent:

Warfare is the greatest affair of state.

Warfare is the Tao of deception.

Although capable, display incapability.

Display profits to entice them.

Attack where they are unprepared.

If they are angry, perturb them.

No country has ever profited from protracted warfare.

The highest realization of warfare is to attack the enemy's plans.

The lowest realization of warfare is to attack fortified cities—generally rephrased today as "Don't become entangled in urban combat."

Attaining one hundred victories in one hundred battles is not the pinnacle of excellence. Subjugating the enemy's army without fighting is the pinnacle of excellence.

One who knows the enemy and himself will not be endangered in a hundred engagements.

First make yourself unconquerable.

Conquer those who are easy to conquer.

The victorious army is like a ton compared with an ounce!

The unorthodox and orthodox mutually produce each other.

Race forth where the enemy does not expect it.

The *ch'i* (*qi*) of the Three Armies can be snatched away.

If you know them and know yourself your victory will not be imperiled.

Cast them into hopeless positions and they will be preserved.

Be tranquil and obscure.

Attack what they love first.

Do not move unless it is advantageous.

Within China's own lengthy and voluminous tradition of military science, the *Art of War* initiated rational speculation upon martial principles and concepts, transforming combat into an art or protoscience rather than a mere exercise in force and brutality. Over the two millennia that subsequently saw the countryside constantly wracked by internal rebellion and external invasion, governments cyclically rise and fall, the population decimated, the infrastructure shattered, and the polity frequently fragmented or submitted to alien occupation, it continued to provide the foundation for tactical and strategic thought and the production of dozens of significant military writings, particularly in the Warring States period and then from the T'ang dynasty onward.

Finally, in the eleventh century A.D., the Sung dynasty, much beset by foreign threats, made it and six other martial works canonical in the hopes that the newly designated compilation known as the *Wu-ching Ch'i-shu (Wujing Qishu)* or *Seven Military Classics*, would preserve and advance China's martial knowledge. Although Sun-tzu's assertions were challenged and modified, they were never ignored; instead, they continuously furnished an ever-renewed starting point for each era's technologically modified and modernized discussions. Despite dramatic changes wrought by advanced explosives, mechanization, air power, logistical transformation, nuclear missiles, digitization, and the rise of information-based warfare, this trend remains much in evidence in the PRC.

The Era of Conflict

Sun-tzu reputedly lived at the end of the Spring and Autumn period (722–481 B.C.E.), an era of dominant personalities and intense multiparty strife when any political or military misstep could doom the state. The semifeudal order imposed by the reigning Chou (Zhou) dynasty in vanquishing its tyrannical predecessor, the Shang, in 1035 B.C.E. had long since declined, and even their ritual authority was now ignored. Dozens of states had dramatically perished, their populaces having been brutally subjugated and their territory annexed. Others continued to survive only through servile submission, adroit political maneuvering, intrigue, assassination, bribery, and constant battling.

Seven of the remaining thirteen significant states— including the southeastern coastal state of Wu, where Sun-tzu apparently plied his persuasions at the end of the sixth century B.C.E.—dominated the realm, the remaining six and various other minor entities constantly being at risk of imminent extinction. Because they all faced multiple threats from contiguous states, more distant enemies, and even nearby steppe and tribal peoples, committing forces to combat invariably entailed enormous risks. Not only could defeat prove fatal, even great victories might significantly debilitate the state, making it unexpectedly vulnerable to surprise attack and easy conquest. The sense of precariousness induced by such turmoil and uncertainty is emphatically captured by the *Art of War*'s very first utterance: "Warfare is the greatest affair of state, the basis of life and death, the Way to survival or extinction."

Although the book never mentions weapons, component forces, or any aspect of military organization, its principles, concepts, and tactics are clearly the product of a specific martial environment and contemporary military practices. A few observations on the nature of Chinese warfare in the late Spring and Autumn and Early Warring states are therefore warranted. But even though the two periods have long been emphatically distinguished by historians, and many aspects of antique practices were changing, the effect was more evolutionary than radical, more continuous than disjunctive. Only after the fourth century B.C.E. when the infantry's mass became overwhelming did their gradual accumulation reach a critical point.

By Sun-tzu's era, the nature, scope, and intensity of warfare had all long been escalating, evolving from limited chariot force clashes on relatively open terrain to extended campaigns undertaken by ever more massive infantry and chariot armies that numbered in the tens of thousands. Chariots have always been identified with early Chinese warfare, but they were not employed by the nobility until at least the middle Shang, after which they gradually grew in quantity and importance. Powered by two horses in combat but lighter and higher than their well-known Roman counterparts, they normally carried three men standing in triangular formation: a driver, a warrior equipped with a crushing weapon, and an archer who doubled as the commander. Through the early Chou, field deployments rarely exceeded a few hundred chariots, but at the Shang's overthrow they were already accompanied by anywhere from ten to twenty-five loosely attached troops.

Dedicated infantry and archery companies, originally about a hundred men each, also appeared in the Shang; campaign armies generally totaled 3,000 men, although they could be augmented by the dispatch of secondary and tertiary forces in similar quantities. As the populace multiplied and their material wealth grew over the centuries, warfare increased in duration, frequency, and scope. Moderate-length Shang campaigns of a few weeks punctuated by brief, single day encounters gradually lengthened to several months, entailing repeated clashes, set-piece deployments, and even stalemates. These tendencies were exacerbated when Chou authority completely collapsed and the newly obstreperous individual states aggressively asserted their independence, targeting clan relations equally with outsiders. Standing forces appeared, the basic army unit grew from 3,000 to 10,000 or 12,500 troops, and expeditionary efforts soon saw two or three indigenous armies combined with several allied contingents in a loosely integrated campaign force.

Chariot numbers also multiplied despite the vehicle's cost, complexity, lengthy production time, and a constant shortage of horses. Witnesses claim that the strongest Spring and Autumn states could easily field a thousand each, with upwards of several thousand being common in the middle Warring States. However, by then foot soldiers had become disproportionately important, having soared to operational concentrations of from 100,000 to 200,000, resulting in enormous command and logistical problems. Moreover, being inherently constrained to level terrain, the chariot proved less effective in peripheral mountainous and wet areas, especially south of the Yangtze and in the states of Wu and Yüeh.

Numerous questions have been raised about the role played by China's light chariots. Although early literature romanticizes chariot clashes and mounted warriors apparently issued personal challenges to each other in the Spring and Autumn period, combat between chariot-based fighters would have been nearly impossible because of instability, the fighting radius of weapons, and limited target acquisition time unless they deliberately halted side by side.

Therefore, by the late Spring and Autumn period the chariot probably functioned primarily as a command and archery platform, mass penetrations and flanking tactics only occasionally being executed. Moreover, their vulnerability required protection by ground troops and therefore coordination between the elements of maneuver and those of persistence, highly difficult to attain and maintain, just as vestiges in the *Art of War* indicate. Nevertheless, they would have permitted the comparatively rapid conveyance of men, and under the direction of a skilled driver and upon reasonable terrain could undoubtedly have been formidable. In addition, an increasingly large number of specialized vehicles, such as supply and assault wagons, also had to be integrated into the army; these in turn complicated the synchronized movement of the campaign components while multiplying the commander's burdens and responsibility. However, the cavalry did not appear as even a minor element until late in the third century, somewhat simplifying the task of coordination.

The growth of massive infantry forces necessarily caused and reflected major changes in civil organization and taxation practices. Increasingly draconian measures were applied at the local level in many areas to bind the people into mutual responsibility units and to ensure that materials could be commandeered and manpower conscripted as required. (Thus the *Art of War* already speaks about six or seven people inconvenienced to support one combat soldier deployed in the field.) As reflected in the book's first chapter, this naturally led to broader questions of training, motivation, and unification because ever greater numbers of people were adversely impacted and many reluctant soldiers found themselves serving for extended periods in hostile environments.

Once in the field, individual warriors were protected by relatively sturdy shields and armor and equipped with either highly sophisticated bows or crushing weapons. Neolithic armor probably consisted solely of animal skins, but leather came to comprise the basic material from the Shang through the end of the Warring States period. When employed in conjunction with shields of wood and leather and coupled with bronze helmets, such armor provided reasonable protection against the weapons and arrowheads of the period. However, as the scope and lethality of conflict intensified, the simple two-piece arrays that formerly covered a soldier's front and back were abandoned for flexible, lamellar tunics fabricated by overlaying multiple small rectangles. Specialized designs also appeared that accommodated the warrior's designated role and function, such as lengthy robes for chariot-mounted fighters.

Bows and (from the middle Warring States onward) crossbows provided the primary weapons for action at a distance; spears apparently having been reserved for close combat rather than for throwing, a tactic that saved the soldier from becoming immediately defenseless. Simple bows date back at least 28,000 years, and numerous ancient skeletons attest that the composite, recurved bows of the Shang and thereafter were powerful enough to penetrate armor and bone. Used in the Early Chou as a criteria for office, skill in archery had long been prized and accuracy out to two hundred yards was normally expected.

Despite the sword's virtually worldwide mystique and contrary to many erroneous Western depictions, the true sword—which might be defined as having a blade length more than double that of the haft and being at least thirty inches long—did not really develop in China until very late in the Spring and Autumn period, and then primarily in the southeastern states of Wu and Yüeh where chariots had limited applicability. Moreover, they were designed for piercing and thrusting rather than for slashing, a function reserved to the comparatively unique weapon known as the *ko* *(ge)*, or dagger-axe, until the advent of sabers near the end of the Warring States period.

Daggers had been carried by archers from the Shang onward as a weapon of last recourse, and although hand and other combat axes date back into the Neolithic period, by the Shang the true field weapon was the dagger-ax. Originally a simple piercing weapon with a three-foot reach created by horizontally affixing a dagger to a long shaft, the dagger-ax was quickly transformed through changes in the blade's curvature, mounting angle, and balance to become a slashing weapon that could effectively target the limbs and neck. Although chariot warriors carried fifteen-foot versions to allow reaching their opponents, foot soldiers were equipped with longer and shorter versions over the centuries.

As the Warring States unfolded, a spear tip was attached at the top of the shaft to remedy vulnerability and constraint problems, thereby converting it into a compound weapon capable of slashing, cutting, thrusting, and stabbing. Specific techniques evolved to exploit this combined potential with sequences that integrated thrusting with reverse undercutting, slashing with reverse thrusting. Although longer versions are shown in the few depictions dating to the period, archaeological remains indicate that the short, three-foot version proliferated during the Warring States period, no doubt because it could be used single-handedly in conjunction with a shield.

Sixth- and fifth-century B.C.E. field armies thus sought to integrate the component forces of chariots and infantry while exploiting various weapons, both in deliberate combination and in dedicated contingents, such as bowmen and unorthodox chariot companies. When deployed in the field and suffering the ongoing changes of combat, this diversity naturally complicated the task of command. Basic organizational structures therefore had to be created and maintained, and control measures that could prove effective whether the army was on the march, encamped, or on the battlefield had to be integrated and imposed.

Early China chose a hierarchical method based upon a multiplier of five and anchored by squads of five men who would be permanently unified and mutually responsible for each other's actions and fate. Five squads were grouped to compose platoons of twenty-five, then companies of 125, brigades of 500 (rather than 625), regiments of 2,500, and finally armies of 12,500. Naturally there were alternative forms and pronounced regional variants, some decade-based, as well as vestigial clan and private forces; but such details became unimportant when commanders confronted and invariably stressed the broader issues of structure and responsiveness.

Simply organizing men into functional units being inadequate, issues of command and control, of maneuver and deployment increasingly came to the fore. No longer could a great noble simply order his clan into battle, lead by example, and courageously participate. Rather, preset deployments had to be developed and the men drilled not just in the complex task of dispersing into formation but also in wielding their weapons effectively and sustaining a coordinated effort. Moreover, their disposition and mode of employment (such as attacking, defending, feinting) had to be inherently flexible and responsive.

Although only a few rudimentary dispositions seem to have existed in Sun-tzu's era, new training methods had to evolve to match their growing complexity. Simultaneously, the chaos of battle demanded communications measures that would allow the commander to exercise active control over his troops by altering their formations and redeploying them as necessary. With the noise—both literal and figurative—and confusion of the highly dynamic combat situation looming large, only simple yet highly visible methods of communication could penetrate the dust and din. Runners and verbal orders, whether written or transmitted by dedicated chains, being doomed to failure, drums, signal fires, colored smoke, flags, gongs, and whistles were all adopted, the men thereafter being rigorously trained in immediate, virtually intuitive response.

Despite constant improvements in systematic defenses that coupled thick, tamped earth fortifications with deep, wide moats and exploited a growing array of countersiege weapons, cities were also evolving into priority targets as a result of their unremitting growth as military, economic, and political centers. Even though the tactics and technology for rapidly reducing them continued to advance, armies that mounted precipitous assaults could still easily be decimated because the well-ensconced defenders enjoyed an almost insurmountable advantage.

In this context of swiftly improving weapons, formations, and skills, all aspects of warfare suddenly demanded scrutiny. Moreover, the "state had to be enriched, the army strengthened" if rulers were not to find themselves easy prey for their foes and friends alike. The commander's character and qualifications necessarily grew critical; neither noble birth nor warrior status was ever again sufficient. Wisdom and experience were deemed vital, and although courage could not be absent, excessive courage could doom an army to defeat. Command techniques, battlefield tactics, and the fundamental concepts necessary to formulate an effective military science all swiftly appeared. Many seem to have originated with Sun-tzu, but others, being the product of sudden strategic insight and long reflection by earlier commanders upon the nature of strife and conflict, clearly preexisted him.

Sun Wu, Man and Myth

It is highly likely that the *Art of War* evolved in the Shandong and Jiangsu region of eastern China, site of the ancient states of Ch'i (*Qi*), Wu, and subsequently

Yüeh during the Spring and Autumn and early Warring States periods. In fact, having been founded
by the semi-legendary T'ai Kung, the great strategist
identified with the Chou's ascendancy over the Shang
and comprehensive (though actually late Warring
States) martial compilation known as the *Liu-t'ao
(Liutao)* or *Six Secret Teachings*, from inception the
state of Ch'i enjoyed a strong military heritage. By
Sun-tzu's era, it had long been an incubator for martial
thought and aggressive political practices. Duke Huan
and Kuan Chung (Guan Zhung), the putative author
of the massive, eclectic work that bears his name,
made Ch'i's history glorious; and Sun Pin (Bin), who
subsequently composed an *Art of War* that adopted
and expanded Sun-tzu's thinking, would serve as a
prominent strategist in Ch'i's two mid-fourth-century
clashes with Wei. Moreover, Sun-tzu himself may have
been from Ch'i even though Wu had well embarked
on a sophisticated military course long before his
appearance.

In comparison with Ch'i's antiquity, Wu and Yüeh
were still in the incipient stages of evolution in the last
century of the Spring and Autumn period. Both enjoyed (or suffered) strong military stimuli from contiguous entities, Wu having intermittently clashed with
Ch'u (Chu) for decades and Yüeh soon battling Wu,
eventually resurging from resounding defeat and near
extinction to exterminate their nemesis in the fifth

century. Accordingly, military knowledge was not just prized, but essential, often being acquired through the itinerant advisors who were beginning to appear. Although Kuan Chung had earlier fulfilled a similar role on personal initiative in Ch'i, the first deliberate martial advisory mission was undertaken by the Duke of Shen in 584 B.C.E. at the behest of Chin (Jin), an old northern power that sought to frustrate Ch'u's plan and intentions (just as Sun-tzu would advocate). A high-ranking Ch'u defector, he was accompanied by a small contingent of troops and a few chariots that were intended to bolster Wu's skills and capabilities. However, because 15 percent of Wu's alluvial terrain consisted of marshes, rivers, and lakes where naval and infantry forces necessarily predominated, the chariot's introduction had little visible impact.

Just before Sun-tzu's appearance, another pivotal Ch'u defector assumed an increasingly prominent role in Wu. Driven by a desire for revenge, the subsequently famous Wu Tzu-hsü (Wu Zixu) futilely tried to persuade King Liao to invade Ch'u before turning to the future King Ho-lü, already a prominent military commander, in frustration. Ho-lü's usurpation of the throne through an assassin introduced by the supposedly righteous Wu Tzu-hsü then set the stage for Sun-tzu's own appearance. Rather than simply being Sun-tzu's mentor, Wu Tzu-hsü recommended him to King Ho-lü solely to advance his own vengeful objectives.

Traditionally identified as the author of the seminal *Ping-fa (Bingfa)* or *Art of War*, Sun Wu or Sun-tzu (Sunzi)—the "tzu" being an honorific marking him as Master Sun—first appeared in this maelstrom about 512 B.C.E. as an itinerant strategist and military advisor. Surprisingly, despite his subsequent fame and the many legends that would surround him throughout imperial Chinese history, Sun-tzu remains an enigma. Because his name never appears in any of the supposedly authentic historical records of the late Spring and Autumn period, his reputation rests solely upon oral transmission and a single incident, and some laudatory words preserved in a brief *Shih Chi (Shi Ji)* biography penned by Ssu-ma Ch'ien (Sima Qian) some four centuries after the event that may have been prompted by the *Art of War*'s popularity in the midst of the Former Han.

Slightly embellished, the *Wu Yüeh Ch'un-ch'iu (Chunqiu)* retells the same incidents in more dramatic form:

> In the third year of Ho-lü's reign as king of Wu, Wu's generals wanted to attack Ch'u but no action was being taken. Wu Tzu-hsü and Po P'i (Bo Pi) spoke with each other: "We nurture officers and make plans on the king's behalf. Because these strategies will be advantageous to the state, the king should attack Ch'u. But he has put off issuing the orders and has no intention of mobilizing the army. What should we do?"

Somewhat later King Ho-lü queried Wu Tzu-hsü and Po P'i: "I want to send forth the army. What do you think?"

Wu-tzu Hsü and Po P'i replied: "We would like to receive the order."

However, the King of Wu secretly thought that the two of them harbored great enmity for Ch'u and deeply feared that they would take the army out only to be exterminated. Ascending his tower, he faced into the southern wind and groaned. A little while later he sighed. None of his ministers understood the king's thoughts. Wu Tzu-hsü secretly realized the king would not make a decision, so he recommended Sun-tzu to him.

Sun-tzu, whose name was Wu, was a native of Wu. Although he excelled at military strategy, as he dwelled in secrecy far away from civilization ordinary people did not recognize his ability. However, being enlightened, wise, and skilled in discrimination, Wu Tzu-hsü knew Sun-tzu could penetrate and destroy the enemy.

One morning while he was discussing military affairs with the king he recommended Sun-tzu seven times. King Ho-lü retorted: "Since you have found several excuses to advance this officer, I want him brought in." He questioned Sun-tzu about military strategy and each time that Sun-tzu laid out a section of his book the king couldn't praise him enough.

Greatly pleased, he inquired: "If possible, I would like to have a minor test of your military strategy."

Sun-tzu replied: "It's possible. We can conduct a minor test with women from the inner palace."

When the king assented, Sun-tzu said: "I would like to have two of your Majesty's beloved concubines each act as commanders for a company."

He ordered all three hundred women to wear helmets and armor, carry swords and shields, and stand. He then instructed them in military methods, that they should advance, withdraw, go left or right, or turn around in accord with the drum. He informed them of the army's prohibitions and then ordered, "At the first beating of the drum you should all assemble, at the second you should advance with your weapons, and at the third deploy into the military formation." At this the palace women all covered their mouths and laughed.

Sun-tzu then personally took up the sticks and beat the drum, giving the orders three times and explaining them five times. They laughed as before. Sun-tzu was enraged when he saw that the women laughed continuously. His eyes suddenly opened wide, his sound was like a terrifying tiger, his hair stood on end under his cap, and his neck broke the tassels at the side. He said to the Master of Laws, "Get the executioner's axes."

Sun-tzu then said: "If the instructions are not clear, the explanations and orders not trusted, it is the general's fault. When they have been instructed three times and the orders have been explained five times, if the troops still do not perform, it is the fault of the officers. What is the procedure according to the rescripts for military discipline?"

The Master of Laws said: "Decapitation!"

Sun-tzu then ordered that the two company commanders, the king's favorite concubines, be beheaded.

King Ho-lü ascended his observation platform just as they were about to behead his beloved concubines. He had an official hasten down to Sun-tzu with orders to say, "I already know that you, my general, are able to command forces. Without these two concubines my food will not be sweet. It would be appropriate not to behead them."

Sun-tzu said: "I have already received my commission as commanding general. According to the rules for generals, when I, as a general, am in command of the army, even though you issue orders to me, I do not have to accept them." He then had them beheaded.

Thereafter when he again beat the drum the women went left and right, advanced and withdrew, and turned around in accord with the prescribed standards without daring to blink an eye. The two companies were completely silent, not daring to look around.

Thereupon Sun-tzu reported to King Ho-lü: "The army is already well ordered. I would like your Majesty to observe them. However you might want to employ them, even sending them forth into fire and water, will not present any difficulty. They can be used to settle All under Heaven."

King Ho-lü, suddenly displeased, said: "I know that you excel at employing the army. Even though I can thereby become a hegemon, there is no place to exercise them. General, please dismiss the army and return to your dwelling. I am unwilling to act further."

Sun-tzu said: "Your Majesty only likes the words, he isn't able to realize their substance."

Wu Tzu-hsü then remonstrated with the king: "I have heard that the army is an inauspicious affair and cannot be wantonly tested. Thus, if someone forms an army but fails to go forth to launch a punitive attack, the Tao of the military will become unclear. Now Your Majesty has been sincerely seeking out talented officers and wants to mobilize the army to execute the brutal state of Ch'u, become hegemon of All under Heaven, and overawe the feudal lords. However, if you do not employ Sun-tzu as your commander, who else can ford the Huai, cross the Ssu (Si), and traverse a thousand kilometers to engage in battle?"

King Ho-lü was elated. He had the drum beaten to convene the army's staff, assembled the troops, and attacked Ch'u. Sun-tzu took Shu, killing the two renegade Wu generals, Princes Kai-yu (Gaiyou) and Chu-yung (Zhuyong).

Ssu-ma Ch'ien concluded by noting that "the king defeated the powerful state of Ch'u in the west, advancing into Ying. He overawed Ch'i (Qi) and Chin (Jin) to the north and manifested his name among the feudal lords. This was due to Sun-tzu imparting power to him." Nevertheless, prompted by certain discrepancies and anachronisms, as well as the improbable story about executing the king's favorite concubines, skeptical scholars have long questioned not only the *Art of War*'s "authenticity" but also its attribution to the historical figure known as Sun Wu. Perhaps the contemporary tendency to disparage the contributions of "great men" in favor of political, economic, and other historical explanations has caused even Sun-tzu's very existence to be increasingly denied and has led to highly acrimonious debates between traditionalists, particularly in the PRC, and scholars aligned with various other schools and interpretations.

Although these highly intriguing questions are historically important, whether the *Art of War* was created by Sun-tzu, the famous Ch'u advisor known as Wu Tzu-hsü, some other anonymous author, a school of martial thought located in Ch'i or Wu, or even Sun Pin in the middle of the deadly Warring States period is irrelevant to its subsequent existence and impact. An early version of the text was certainly circulating late in the fourth century B.C.E.; thereafter, its teachings quickly became the tactical and conceptual basis for the burgeoning military studies necessitated by the ever more lethal strife of the Warring States period and subsequent contemplations by strategists and commanders during the imperial period. Even though the book has been variously called *Sun-tzu's Art of War*, the *Art of War*, or just *Sun-tzu* (because each chapter originally opened with "Sun-tzu said"), the book's inception has always been associated with Sun-tzu and the dramatic, indelible image of the palace women's executions. Accordingly, throughout our discussions we have adopted the conventional means of referring to the author (or authors) as "Sun-tzu," although with full consciousness of alternative possibilities.

Nature of the Work

Irrespective of the actual author, the *Art of War* evolved in the general milieu of the late Spring and Autumn and early Warring States period when, perhaps in response to the verve of the period, systematic philosophic thought first evolved and the first overt instructors appeared, epitomized by Confucius, who has traditionally been venerated as China's first teacher. In

fact, Confucius and Sun-tzu, the paragons of the virtuous and martial approaches respectively, were contem-
poraries, both having flourished at the end of the sixth
and early fifth centuries. Moreover, the *Analects*—the
famous compendium of sayings attributed to Confucius
himself but now known to have been substantially
composed subsequent to his death—and the *Art of War*
equally consist of a series of laconic pronouncements
on a variety of discrete topics, cobbled together under
chapter headings marked only by tangential relationships with the contents. For example, a typical and
well-known saying preserved in the *Analects* states,
"Don't be troubled that other men do not know you,
be concerned that you do not know other men." Thus,
despite their widely acknowledged profundity and voluminous explications by subsequent commentators,
readers have regarded many of them as enigmatic, con-
fusing, and even impenetrable for nearly twenty-five
centuries.

This esoteric, often frustrating sense of disjuncture
stems in part from the verbal teaching practices of the
late Spring and Autumn and early Warring States.
Memorized materials generally formed the basis for discussion and the master's pronouncements were expected to be precisely remembered for subsequent
transmission and contemplation. (Numerical rubrics
that facilitate memorization and recall, such as "five"
categories or "nine" terrains, no doubt reflect this oral

emphasis.) The *Art of War* also incorporates battlefield wisdom, observational notes, and formulaic pronouncements apparently derived from centuries of combat experience. Although memorizing lengthy passages was not completely precluded, the instruction's extemporaneous nature favored the succinct summaries that are just as visible in the Buddha's early pronouncements.

More important, apart from the occasional silk roll, until paper made its first appearance in the Later Han the recording medium consisted of narrow bamboo strips, generally a foot or slightly more in length, that could hold between fifteen and thirty brush-written Chinese characters. Laboriously produced and highly inconvenient, they had to be strung together with thin cords to create paragraphs, chapters, and then books that would be rolled up for storage or carrying. (A single "book" might need two or three such rolls, while three such books would require a wheelbarrow to transport.) Because each strip basically functioned as the equivalent of a modern note card, to a considerable extent both the *Analects* and the *Art of War* can be considered collections of "prompts" or "cribs" that capture the essence of a subject, materials to be expanded in the process of instruction and discussion.

Certain topics required two or more strips, others were revisited over time, whether because of queries or because the master summarized the material differently, adding insights and providing new perspectives. Some of the strips may also have been used individually rather than immediately bound up, adding to the complexity of the final integration. With practice, the medium's inconveniences became tolerated, and by the middle of the fourth century B.C.E. true paragraphs were appearing in works such as the *Mencius* as well as the *Tso Chuan*, China's first historical narrative, increasingly lengthy disquisitions quickly following.

Some observations from our own reconstruction of a bamboo *Art of War* three decades ago that required nearly three hundred strips may prove illuminating. Despite the project's being undertaken solely by native Chinese speakers, the process proved tedious, frustrating, and troublesome, all annoyances that would be multiplied during the composing or writing of an original over weeks or months in comparison with merely copying an extant book. Once the ink dried, maintaining order among the completed strips should have been simplicity itself; but when more than a few accumulated, they frequently became disordered by being moved and shuffled about, requiring further effort to reorganize. Similar problems no doubt faced ancient readers when the bindings failed or a "book" was retied, not to mention the scholars who reconstructed the *Art of War*, *Sun Pin's Military Methods*, and the other pre-Ch'in writings from the disheveled piles of Han dynasty tomb slips that are now revealing so much about the culture and history of the Warring States.

Whatever writings Confucius and Sun-tzu may have bequeathed, their immediate disciples and numerous compilers subsequently edited and reedited the collections, sometimes expanding, excising, rearranging, and generally "improving" the material. This practice continued even after the introduction of paper in the Han, the great Three Kingdoms general Ts'ao Ts'ao (Cao Cao), the first known commentator, now being vilified for fatally damaging the *Art of War* when he reportedly reduced it from eighty-two chapters to just thirteen. (However, other traditions, some tomb fragments, and the *Shih Chi* biography all imply that the work consisted of just thirteen sections when first presented, and just such a text clearly circulated early in the Han.)

At least in the *Analects*, layers and even chapters of extensive material were subsequently added, and a few accretions reputedly reflecting the conflict levels and practices of the Warring States can arguably be discerned in the *Art of War*. Some of Sun-tzu's discussions, being remarkably systematic and coherent, would certainly have required two or three strips, suggesting either a slightly later stage of composition or subsequent expansion. At the same time, so-called classical Chinese being extremely condensed, a single strip may be sufficient to compress a discussion that sprawls across several lengthy English sentences.

Not unexpectedly, despite extensive scrutiny and reshaping over the centuries, whether beneficial or detrimental, the author's original intent was often muddied by these editors, compilers, and commentators, particularly because the language continued to evolve and earlier meanings changed or were forgotten. Accordingly, even though nominal connectors such as "thus" and "therefore" repeatedly appear, contiguous sentences often lack continuity, the *Art of War* frequently appears bereft of systemic thinking, and parts may strike the most astute reader as mutually contradictory. However, careful reading and pondering within the larger context of the Warring States and the subsequent Chinese military corpus reveal that a dramatic core vision underlies the entire text, that the *Art of War* is an organic whole displaying multiple links between its many parts, and that the concrete contents can be rendered understandable by unpacking the compressed text and systematically explicating the pronouncements in terms of that vision, thereby emphasizing their role in achieving greater objectives. This is the intent of our chapter notes and the afterword's broader contemplation of selected core concepts and their possible relevance in the contemporary world.

1

始
計 *Initial Estimations*

Warfare is the greatest affair of state, the basis of life and death, the Tao (Dao) for survival or extinction. It must be thoroughly pondered and analyzed. Therefore, structure it according to the following five factors, comparatively evaluate it through estimation, and seek out its true nature. The first is termed the Tao, the second Heaven, the third Earth, the fourth generals, and the fifth the laws for military organization and discipline.

The Tao causes the people to be fully in accord with the ruler. Thus they will die with him, they will live with him and not fear danger.

Heaven encompasses *yin* and *yang*, cold and heat, the constraints of the seasons, according with and going contrary to, the basis of victory in warfare.

Earth encompasses high or low, far or near, difficult or easy, expansive or confined ground, fatal or tenable terrain.

The general encompasses wisdom, credibility, be-nevolence, courage, and strictness.

The laws for military organization and discipline encompass organization and regulations, the Tao of command, and the management of logistics.

There are no generals who have not heard of these five. Those who understand them will be victorious, those who do not understand them will not be victorious.

Thus, when making a comparative assessment through estimation, seeking out the true nature, ask:

Which ruler has the Tao?

Which general has greater ability?

Who has gained the advantages of Heaven and Earth?

Whose laws and orders are more thoroughly im-plemented?

Whose forces are stronger?

Whose officers and troops are better trained?

Whose rewards and punishments are clearer?

From these we will know victory and defeat!

Generals who follow my methods for estimation, if employed, will certainly be victorious and should be retained. Generals who do not follow my methods for estimation, if employed, will certainly be defeated, so dismiss them.

After assessing the advantages in accord with what you have heard, put them into effect with strategic power supplemented by field tactics that respond to external factors. Strategic power stems from controlling the tactical imbalance of power in accord with the gains to be realized.

Warfare is the Tao of deception. Thus:

Although you are capable, display incapability.

When committed to employing your forces, feign inactivity.

When your objective is nearby, make it appear distant.

When your objective is far away, make it appear nearby.

Display profits to entice them.

Create disorder and take them.

If they are substantial, prepare for them.

If they are strong, avoid them.

If they are angry, perturb them.

Be deferential to foster their arrogance.

If they are rested, force them to exert themselves.

If they are united, cause them to be separated.

Attack where they are unprepared.

Go forth where they will not expect it.

These are the ways military strategists are victorious. They cannot be spoken of in advance.

Before the engagement, those who determine in the ancestral temple that they will be victorious have found that the majority of factors are in their favor. Before the engagement, those who determine in the ancestral temple that they will not be victorious have found few factors are in their favor.

If those who find that the majority of factors favor them will be victorious while those who have found few factors favor them will be defeated, what about someone who finds no factors in his favor?

When observed from this perspective, victory and defeat will be apparent.

○   ○   ○

Having been composed in an era of incessant and increasingly lethal strife when one misstep could doom a state to extinction, the *Art of War* not only opens with a bold statement about the crucial importance of warfare but also converts its practice into an art or a science rather than into an extemporaneous enterprise prompted by desire or emotion. Although five factors are recognized as fundamental, and several others, often paired, are enumerated throughout the text, the very act of isolating and identifying a limited number makes assessment—the weighing of the relative strengths and weaknesses for both sides—possible; therefore, a calculated, rational approach can be taken when initiating combat and every other enterprise.

As would be expected during an era whose turbulence demanded unceasing efforts at strengthening the administration and augmenting the state, the Tao of government receives priority. (An elusive and oft nebulous term, *tao (dao)* basically means "way" or "road," though its connotations embrace the patterns or principles of various important natural and human phenomena, the "way things are.") Questions of strategy and other critical issues, such as logistics, are deferred, the unity of the people, the very basis of warfare, instead being stressed.

Japanese commentators often raise the example of the measures Hitler took in uniting Germany before World War II as an example of its importance, though their own draconian techniques for instilling fanatical belief among their largely homogeneous populace in the 1930s might equally be cited. Although the late twentieth-century PRC provides another, more recent instance, the most dramatic contemporary implementation (apart from Islamic insurgency movements) has unquestionably occurred in North Korea, where reportedly 90 percent of the downtrodden inhabitants enthusiastically support the government and their forthcoming war with the United States. Conversely, the Vietnam conflict surely attests to the pernicious effects of disunity, of the ruler's failing to achieve the people's accord.

"Initial Estimations" also introduces two quintessential concepts: deception is critical to warfare and the enemy should always be manipulated in order to wrest victory at the lowest cost. Varied and ingenious deceptive measures furnish key means for misleading and befuddling the enemy, the fourteen enumerated in the chapter being among the concrete techniques capable of accomplishing this goal.

Finally, Sun-tzu's dictum "Attack where they are unprepared, go forth where they will not expect it" not only became a watchword for Chinese military science, but has also been adopted in many realms and entered the very language itself.

作
戦 *2*

Waging War

In general, the strategy for employing the military is this: If there are one thousand four-horse attack chariots, one thousand leather armored support chariots, one hundred thousand mailed troops, and provisions are transported one thousand *li*, then the domestic and external campaign expenses, the expenditures for advisors and guests, materials such as glue and lacquer, and providing chariots and armor will be one thousand pieces of gold per day. Only then can an army of one hundred thousand be mobilized.

When employing them in battle, a victory that is long in coming will blunt their weapons and dampen their ardor. If you attack cities, their strength will be exhausted. If you expose the army to a prolonged campaign, the state's resources will be inadequate.

When their weapons have grown dull and their spirits depressed, when our strength has been expended and resources consumed, then the feudal lords will take advantage of our exhaustion to arise. Even though you have wise generals, they will not be able to achieve a good result.

Thus, in military campaigns, I have heard of awkward speed but have never seen any skill in lengthy campaigns. No country has ever profited from protracted warfare.

Those who do not thoroughly comprehend the dangers inherent in employing the army are incapable of truly knowing the potential advantages of military actions.

One who excels in employing the military does not conscript the people twice nor transport provisions a third time. If you obtain your equipment from within the state and rely on seizing provisions from the enemy, the army's foodstuffs will be sufficient.

The state is impoverished by the army when it transports provisions far off. When provisions are transported far off, the hundred surnames are impoverished. Those in proximity to the army will sell their goods expensively. When goods are expensive, the hundred surnames' wealth will be exhausted. When their wealth is exhausted, they will be extremely hard-pressed to supply their village's military impositions.

When their strength has been expended and their wealth depleted, then the houses in the central plains will be empty. The expenses of the hundred surnames will be some seven-tenths of whatever they have. The ruler's irrecoverable expenditures, such as ruined chariots, exhausted horses, armor, helmets, arrows and crossbows, halberd-tipped and spear-tipped large, movable protective shields, village oxen and large wagons, will consume six-tenths of his resources.

Thus the wise general will concentrate on securing provisions from the enemy. One bushel of the enemy's foodstuffs is worth twenty of ours, one picul of fodder is worth twenty of ours.

Anger motivates men to slay the enemy, material goods stimulate them to seize profits from the enemy. Thus when ten or more chariots are captured in chariot encounters, reward the first to get one. Change their flags and pennants to ours, intermix and employ them with our own chariots. Treat captured soldiers well in order to nurture them for our own use. This is referred to as "conquering the enemy and growing stronger."

The army values being victorious, it does not value prolonged warfare. Therefore, a general who understands warfare is Master of Fate for the people, ruler of the state's security or endangerment.

o   o   o

By the Warring States period it had become obvious that military activities were bankrupting even the strongest states and decimating their manpower. Not only did lengthy commitments exhaust the troops and make them susceptible to defeat but extensive expeditions created irreversible power vacuums that contiguous, rapacious enemies might readily exploit. Although the forcible acquisition of wealth and materials and the battlefield annexation of territory and populace could ameliorate the losses, the gains of victory often proved difficult to consolidate. Sun-tzu therefore stressed that prolonged warfare must be avoided, that rulers should not be seduced by combat's illusory glory.

Logistical problems have always plagued field armies, particularly those operating in remote areas and outstripping their supply lines. Ancient Chinese commanders struggled to supplement their initial provisions with ongoing shipments, local purchases, foraging, plundering, and seizures from the enemy. Although deliberate confiscation policies have become outmoded by mechanized transport, astute troops have always gathered weapons, ammunition, and foodstuffs whenever possible; indeed, Soviet operational practice sometimes emphasized such opportunistic acquisition, at least for selected units.

Normally, the very existence of guerrilla and insurgent forces similarly hinges upon forcibly acquiring materials, provisions, and weapons. Accordingly, Mao Tse-tung made it a basic tenet of the Communist strategy for defeating Japanese forces and the Kuomintang, though without citing the *Art of War*. (A "war of annihilation" was conducted against isolated Japanese units but not the massive KMT forces because the latter were viewed as being composed mainly of disaffected peasants who might be converted to the Communist cause, just as in traditional China.)

Compelling men not just to overcome their fear but to face the horrors of combat willingly (or to engage in other risky enterprises) and fight fervently has always posed a great challenge. Basing their logic on several crucial passages in the *Art of War*, including "anger motivates men to slay the enemy, material goods stimulate them to wrest profits or advantage," Warring States military thinkers developed a sophisticated theory of motivation and control. However, the fear of punishment coupled with mutual responsibility (i.e., "entanglement"), techniques that encompassed the coercive threat of family execution, generally received emphasis, victory providing the only opportunity to plunder and profit extensively.

Finally, it should be noted that despite Sun-tzu's adamant opposition to recklessly engaging in battle and to prolonged warfare, military engagements might still entail a potential for profit. Nevertheless, embarking on warfare always requires careful assessment, well-pondered plans, and a thorough comprehension of "the dangers inherent in employing the army."

謀攻 3

Planning Offensives

In general, the method for employing the military is this: Preserving the enemy's state capital is best, destroying their state capital second best. Preserving their army is best, destroying their army second best. Preserving their battalions is best, destroying their battalions second best. Preserving their companies is best, destroying their companies second best. Preserving their squads is best, destroying their squads second best.

For this reason, attaining one hundred victories in one hundred battles is not the pinnacle of excellence. Subjugating the enemy's army without fighting is the true pinnacle of excellence.

Thus the highest realization of warfare is to attack the enemy's plans; next is to attack their alliances; next to attack their army; and the lowest is to attack their fortified cities.

This tactic of attacking fortified cities is adopted only when unavoidable. Preparing large movable protective shields, armored assault wagons, and other equipment and devices will require three months. Building offensive earthworks will require another three months to complete. If the general cannot overcome his impatience but instead launches an assault wherein his men swarm over the walls like ants, he will kill one third of his officers and troops and the city will still not be taken. This is the disaster that results from attacking fortified cities.

Thus one who excels at employing the military subjugates other people's armies without engaging in battle, captures other people's fortified cities without attacking them, and destroys other people's states without prolonged fighting. He must fight under Heaven with the paramount aim of "preservation." Thus his weapons will not become dull and the gains can be preserved. This is the strategy for planning offensives.

In general, the strategy for employing the military is this: If your strength is ten times theirs, surround them; if five, then attack them; if double, then divide your forces. If you are equal in strength to the enemy, you can engage them. If fewer, you can circumvent them. If outmatched, you can avoid them. A small enemy that acts inflexibly will become the captives of a large enemy.

The general is the supporting pillar of state. If his talents are all-encompassing, the state will invariably be strong. If the supporting pillar is marked by fissures, the state will invariably grow weak.

There are three ways by which an army is put into difficulty by a ruler:

He does not know that the Three Armies should not advance but instructs them to advance, or does not know that the Three Armies should not withdraw and orders them to retreat. This is termed "entangling the army."

He does not understand the Three Armies' military affairs but directs them in the same way as his civil administration. Then the officers will become confused.

He does not understand the Three Armies' tactical balance of power but undertakes responsibility for command. Then the officers will be doubtful.

When the Three Armies are already confused and doubtful, the danger of the feudal lords taking advantage of the situation arises. This is referred to as "a disordered army drawing another on to victory."

Thus there are five factors from which victory can be known:

Those who know when they can fight and when they cannot fight will be victorious.

Those who recognize how to employ large and small numbers will be victorious.

Those whose upper and lower ranks have the same desires will be victorious.

Those who, fully prepared, await the unprepared will be victorious.

Those whose generals are capable and not interfered with by the ruler will be victorious.

These five are the Tao for knowing victory.

Thus it is said that in warfare, those who know the enemy and know themselves will not be endangered in a hundred engagements. Those who do not know the enemy but know themselves will sometimes be victorious, sometimes meet with defeat. Those who know neither the enemy nor themselves will invariably be defeated in every engagement.

o   o   o

The chapter's initial passages succinctly advance a view of offensive warfare consonant with Sun-tzu's assertion that victory should be swiftly achieved at minimal cost. Enemies should be subjugated by frustrating their plans, thwarting their preparations, or undermining their alliances, thereby augmenting the state and increasing its awesomeness. Thus, despite the historically attested Chinese practice of brutally resolving conflicts, the conclusion that "attaining one hundred victories in one hundred battles is not the pinnacle of excellence; subjugating the enemy's army without fighting is the true pinnacle of excellence" not only became a well-known measure for appraising behavior but also continues to be an essential principle of modern PRC doctrine. Moreover, attacking plans and alliances is crucial to the contemporary quest of thwarting irregular forces.

Should combat become inevitable, commanders must still strive to minimize the destruction they inflict even as they decisively wrest victory, thereby maximizing the battlefield gains while preserving the infrastructure and diminishing potential enmity. Across the centuries, however, "fighting with the aim of preservation" generally remained mere theorization. Instead, China repeatedly witnessed the vengeful destruction of entire cities and unimaginable carnage as troops, civilians, and even prisoners were slaughtered en masse.

The corollary to attacking plans is avoiding stupid assaults on fortified positions because the ensconced defense usually enjoyed virtually insurmountable advantages. Despite the deliberate bombing of major cities during World War II, the idea that "the lowest strategy is to attack fortified cities" retains relevance, though it is generally—albeit incorrectly—interpreted as an admonition to avoid combat on urban terrain fraught with obstacles and danger for regular troops.

The increasing complexities of Spring and Autumn warfare saw a shift from royally commanded ad hoc contingents to more professionally led standing armies. As rulers became more effete and estranged from the realities of combat, the dramatically different temperament and values appropriate to the civil and martial spheres inevitably engendered clashes between elite court members and brusque military specialists. Communication difficulties that fundamentally prevented the ruler from reacting to the rapidly evolving battle in a meaningful way also compounded the problem. Thus it is hardly surprising that Sun-tzu stridently decried any interference with the field commander's power.

The final pronouncement, another that affected the mindset and values of a hundred generations, is a clear injunction to be as vigorous in self-scrutiny as in examining others. Failing to be objective, to recognize weakness as well as strength when predicting enemy actions and probable combat results, not only leads to error and delusion, but also catastrophic failure.

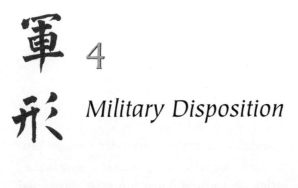

4

Military Disposition

In antiquity, those who excelled in warfare first made themselves unconquerable in order to await the moment when the enemy could be conquered.

Being unconquerable lies with yourself, being conquerable lies with the enemy. Therefore, those who excel in warfare are able to make themselves unconquerable, but cannot necessarily cause the enemy to be conquerable.

Thus it is said that a strategy for conquering the enemy can be known but yet not possible to implement.

Those who cannot be victorious assume a defensive posture, those who can be victorious attack. In these circumstances, by assuming a defensive posture strength will be more than adequate, whereas in offensive actions it would be inadequate.

Those who excel at defense bury themselves away below the lowest depths of Earth. Those who excel at offense move from above the greatest heights of Heaven. Thus they are able to preserve themselves and attain complete victory.

Perceiving a victory that does not surpass what the masses could know is not the pinnacle of excellence. Wresting victories for which All under Heaven proclaim your excellence is not the pinnacle of excellence.

Thus lifting an autumn hair cannot be considered great strength; seeing the sun and moon cannot be considered acute vision; hearing the sound of thunder cannot be considered having sensitive ears. Those that the ancients referred to as excelling at warfare conquered those who were easy to conquer. Thus the victories of those who excelled in warfare were not marked by fame for wisdom or courageous achievement. Thus their victories were free from errors. One who is free from errors directs his measures toward certain victory, conquering those who are already defeated.

Thus those who excel at warfare first establish themselves in a position where they cannot be defeated while not losing any opportunity to defeat the enemy. For this reason, victorious armies first realize the conditions for victory and then seek to engage in battle. Vanquished armies fight first and then seek victory.

Those who excel at employing the military cultivate the Tao and preserve the laws; therefore, they are able to be the regulators of victory and defeat.

As for military methods: The first is termed measurement; the second, estimation of forces; the third, calculation of numbers of men; the fourth, weighing relative strength; and the fifth, victory.

Terrain gives birth to measurement; measurement produces the estimation of forces. Estimation of forces gives rise to calculating the numbers of men. Calculating the numbers of men gives rise to weighing strength. Weighing strength gives birth to victory.

Thus the victorious army is like a ton compared with an ounce, while the defeated army is like an ounce weighed against a ton! The combat of the victorious is like the sudden release of a pent-up torrent down a thousand-fathom gorge. This is the strategic disposition of force.

o   o   o

Ignoring the dubious saying that "the best defense is an aggressive offense," a workable strategy for surviving the repeated onslaughts of elusive, irregular forces is perhaps contained in the dictum "Being unconquerable lies with yourself, being conquerable lies with the enemy. Thus one who excels in warfare is able to make himself unconquerable, but cannot necessarily cause the enemy to be conquerable." As previously asserted, substantial forces should therefore be avoided, or at least well prepared for.

Adopting an unconquerable posture is premised upon military combat's being an art or science rather than a blind exercise in valor. In accord with the assessment procedures already outlined, measurement and estimation are required in every situation so that appropriate force levels can be correlated with the enemy's strength, the topography, and the immediate objectives. Moreover, the terrain's configuration constrains the tactical possibilities and predisposes the ground to certain modes of action and methods of exploitation. Accordingly, "measurement" refers not just to the terrain's expanse but also to its tactical classification; "estimation" encompasses the types of component forces, troop levels, and quantities of provisions and materials required to sustain a campaign or battle. (Because topography is a critical concept in early Chinese military thought, subsequent chapters describe the features and articulate the tactical possibilities for numerous categories of terrain.)

Although astutely exploiting topographical advantages and adopting a strongly fortified defense, thereby forcing opponents to mount foolhardy attacks—"to fight first and then seek victory"—make it possible to avoid defeat and extinction, they do not guarantee that the enemy can be vanquished. Commanders should employ appropriate measures to manipulate and debilitate the opponents, but equally important are command and control techniques that fully realize the army's potential and utilize advantageous terrain to simply overwhelm the enemy with "strategic power." (The concept of "strategic power," explicated at length in upcoming sections, combines raw power with positional and other combat multipliers, ensuing that the enemy cannot escape the circumstances of their fate.) Then, at the appropriate moment, "the victorious army will be like a ton compared with an ounce, the combat of the victorious like the sudden release of a pent-up torrent down a thousand-fathom gorge" and no "opportunity to defeat the enemy" will be lost.

Finally, although the chapter sets a rigorous tone, a certain esotericism marks the commander's unfathomable wisdom and strategy. Once achieved, his victories seem ordinary, but only because his acumen, operational tactics, preliminary preparations, and manipulation of the enemy all combined to create the possibility of victory and make their conquest inevitable.

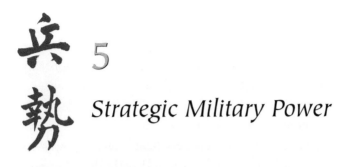

5

Strategic Military Power

In general, commanding a large number is like commanding a few. It is a question of dividing up the numbers. Fighting with a large number is like fighting with a few. It is a question of configuration and designation.

What enable the masses of the Three Armies to invariably withstand the enemy without being defeated are the unorthodox and orthodox.

If, wherever the army attacks, it is like a whetstone thrown against an egg, it is due to the vacuous and substantial.

In general, in battle one engages with the orthodox and gains victory through the unorthodox. Thus those who excel at sending forth the unorthodox are as inexhaustible as Heaven and Earth, as unlimited as the Yangtze and Yellow Rivers.

What reach an end and begin again are the sun and moon. What die and are reborn are the four seasons.

The notes do not exceed five, but the changes of the five notes can never be fully heard. The colors do not exceed five, but the changes of the five colors can never be completely seen. The flavors do not exceed five, but the changes of the five flavors can never be completely tasted.

In warfare, the strategic configurations of power do not exceed the unorthodox and orthodox, but the changes of the unorthodox and orthodox can never be completely exhausted. The unorthodox and orthodox mutually produce each other, just like an endless cycle. Who can exhaust them?

The strategic configuration of power is visible in the onrush of pent-up water tumbling stones along. The effect of constraints is visible in the onrush of a bird of prey breaking the bones of its target.

Thus the strategic configuration of power of those who excel in warfare is sharply focused, their constraints are precise. Their strategic configuration of power is like a fully drawn crossbow, their constraints like the release of the trigger.

Intermixed and turbulent, the fighting appears chaotic, but they cannot be made disordered. In turmoil and confusion, their deployment is circular and they cannot be defeated.

Simulated chaos is given birth from control; the illusion of fear is given birth from courage; feigned weakness is given birth from strength. Order and disorder are a question of numbers; courage and fear are a question of the strategic configuration of power; strength and weakness are a question of the deployment of forces.

Those who excel at moving the enemy deploy in a configuration to which the enemy must respond. They offer something that the enemy must seize. With profit they move them, with the foundation they await them.

Thus those who excel at warfare seek victory through the strategic configuration of power, not from reliance on men. Thus they are able to select men and employ strategic power.

Those who employ strategic power command men in battle as if they were rolling logs and stones. The nature of wood and stone is to be quiet when stable but to move when on precipitous ground. If they are square they stop, if round they tend to move. Thus the strategic power of those who excel at employing men in warfare is comparable to rolling round boulders down a thousand-fathom mountain. Such is the strategic configuration of power.

o   o   o

"Strategic power," the central concept of this chapter, is closely intertwined and essentially created by the orthodox and unorthodox. They in turn become possible through the imposition of regulation and control, through the training and discipline that allow the army to segment and reform, to maintain order within the swirl of battle, to create a facade of chaos, or to mount a feigned retreat, flexibly and decisively responding as directed. Only thereafter may the enemy be manipulated to advantage, gaps in their defenses created and exploited, and a rapid conquest achieved by employing the substantial against the newly vacuous.

Numerous terms have been used to approximate the concept of *shih* (*shi*), the term translated as "strategic configuration of power" or, more succinctly, "strategic power." Not simply an indication of brute strength or raw power, it is in essence a comparative term that emphasizes a tactical imbalance in the forces confronting each other coupled with advantages derived from their relative positions on the terrain, such as commanding the heights or being compressed into a ravine. Astutely deploying into configurations that maximize the army's leverage while exploiting deliberately induced weaknesses results in an overwhelming application of firepower, analogous to the sudden onrush of pent-up water cascading down from a mountain peak or "a whetstone thrown against an egg." Precision, constraint, and measure are nonetheless required to realize the full potential of strategic power in the shortest interval and to avoid squandering hard-won advantages.

The unorthodox and orthodox, an interdependent conceptual pair crucial to Chinese military doctrine first articulated in this single *Art of War* passage, are integral to creating the conditions for an unexpected but highly constrained onslaught. Just as the English word "unorthodox" implies, in contrast to "orthodox" tactics that employ troops in normal, conventional, "by the book" and therefore predictable ways, "unorthodox" (*ch'i/qi*) tactics stress flexibility, imagination, and surprise. However, although they are initially dependent upon normal expectation within a particular context, the orthodox and unorthodox are situationally defined and inherently constrained by an opponent's ongoing assessment rather than inalterably fixed.

Being a pair in polar tension, mutually defining, mutually transforming, and circular in essence, normally orthodox measures may be exploited in unorthodox ways. Similarly, with repeated usage or because they have been anticipated, unorthodox attacks may become orthodox; this can lead not only to chains of projecting and countering, to "I know that you know that I know" games carried to two or three levels but also to stupefying self-delusion and paralyzing psychological complexity.

6

Vacuity and Substance

In general, those who occupy the battleground first and await the enemy will be at ease; those who occupy the battleground afterward and must race to the conflict will be fatigued. Thus those who excel at warfare compel men and are not compelled by other men.

In order to cause the enemy to come of their own volition, extend some apparent profit. In order to prevent the enemy from coming forth, show them potential harm.

Thus, if the enemy is rested, you can tire them; if they are well fed, you can make them hungry; if they are at rest, you can move them.

Go forth to positions to which they must race. Race forth where they do not expect it.

To travel a thousand *li* without becoming fatigued, traverse unoccupied terrain. To ensure taking the objective in an attack, strike positions that are undefended. To be certain of an impregnable defense, secure positions that the enemy will not attack.

Thus, when someone excels in attacking, the enemy does not know where to mount their defense; when someone excels at defense, the enemy does not know where to attack. Subtle! Subtle! It approaches the formless. Spiritual! Spiritual! It attains the soundless. Therefore you can be the enemy's Master of Fate.

To effect an unhampered advance, strike their vacuities. To effect a retreat that cannot be overtaken, employ unmatchable speed. Thus if I want to engage in combat, even though the enemy has high ramparts and deep moats, they cannot avoid doing battle because I attack objectives they must rescue.

If I do not want to engage in combat, even though I merely draw a line on the ground and defend it, they will not be able to engage us in battle because we thwart their movements.

If we can determine the enemy's disposition of forces while we have no perceptible form, we can concentrate our forces while the enemy is fragmented. If we are concentrated into a single force while they are fragmented into ten, then we attack them with ten times their strength. Thus we are many and the enemy few. If we can attack their few with our many, those whom we engage in battle will be severely constrained.

The location where we will engage the enemy must not become known to them. If it is not known, then the positions they must prepare to defend will be numerous. If the positions the enemy prepares to defend are numerous, then the forces we will engage will be few.

Thus, if they prepare to defend the front, to the rear there will be few men. If they defend the rear, in the front there will be few. If they prepare to defend the left flank, then on the right there will be few men. If they prepare to defend the right flank, then on the left there will be few men. If no position is left undefended, no position will have more than a few.

The few are the ones who prepare against others; the many are the ones who make others prepare against them.

If you know the field of battle and know the day of battle, you can traverse a thousand *li* and assemble to engage in combat. If you do not know the field of battle nor know the day for battle, then the left flank cannot aid the right nor the right flank aid the left; the front cannot aid the rear nor the rear aid the front. How much more so when the distant are some tens of *li* away and the near several *li* apart?

As I analyze it, even though Yüeh's army is numerous, of what great advantage is it to them for attaining victory? Thus I say victory can be achieved. Even though the enemy is more numerous, they can be forced not to fight.

Critically analyze them to know the estimations for gain and loss. Stimulate them to know their patterns of movement and stopping. Determine their disposition of force to learn the tenable and fatal terrain. Probe them to know where they have an excess, where an insufficiency.

The pinnacle of military deployment approaches the formless. If it is formless, then neither can the deepest spy discern it nor the wise make plans against it.

In accord with the enemy's disposition we impose measures on the masses that produce victory, but the masses are unable to fathom them. Men all know the disposition by which we attain victory, but no one knows the configuration through which we control the victory. Thus a victorious battle strategy is not repeated, the configurations of response to the enemy are inexhaustible.

Now the army's disposition of force is like water. Water's configuration avoids heights and races downward. The army's disposition of force avoids the substantial and strikes the vacuous. Water configures its flow in accord with the terrain, the army controls its victory in accord with the enemy. Thus the army does not maintain any constant strategic configuration of power, water has no constant shape. One who is able to change and transform in accord with the enemy and wrest victory is termed "spiritual." Thus none of the five phases constantly dominates; the four seasons do not have constant positions; the sun shines for longer and shorter periods; and the moon wanes and waxes.

○ ○ ○

This chapter is titled "Vacuity and Substance" because key sentences reiterate the concept of exploiting voids in the enemy's deployment while not becoming entangled with substantial forces. However, it commences with a dictum of universal applicability, a virtual cornerstone of Sun-tzu's doctrine: "Those who excel at warfare compel men and are not compelled by men." Accordingly, the discussion focuses upon the means and measures for seizing the initiative, forcing the enemy into a passive role, shaping the field of conflict, and achieving a surpassing, localized advantage wherein one's own strategic power, however limited, can have an overwhelming impact.

Previous sections have already emphasized the importance of manipulating the enemy, of luring them into movement so that they may be frustrated, fatigued, destabilized, surprised, and then efficiently attacked. "Vacuity and Substance" not only advises armies to achieve unimpeded movement and mount devastating strikes by discovering and using undefended terrain but also advocates the active creation of the necessary gaps and vacuities. This task should be accomplished by obfuscating the enemy, rendering and keeping them ignorant, thereby compelling them to compensate for their uncertainty by multiplying their deployments and diffusing their defensive efforts. Given that the befuddled enemy can field only a finite number of troops, the resulting dispersal guarantees at least a few relatively unguarded areas that can readily be penetrated by locally concentrated forces.

Although feints, deception, and enticements are frequently employed to achieve this objective, "Vacuity and Substance" advances the even more transcendent idea of being "formless" and therefore unfathomable. Not only should the army be unknowable but the commander's plans and intent should be kept secret, both before and after execution. Moreover, rather than constantly relying upon proven but discernible tactics, the commander must vary previously successful methods, even abandon them to prevent them from becoming predictable. Naturally, the commander's strategy cannot be completely independent of certain realities, such as the enemy's strength and disposition, but within the situational possibilities flexibility should remain the rule.

Finally, it must be realized that no matter how successful they are, these measures and techniques cannot ensure combat victory without devoting a corresponding effort to fathoming and assessing the enemy. The battlefield must be anticipated, the enemy's deployments known, and their capabilities determined not just by observation but by active probing as well. Although historically accomplished by reconnaissance forces that deliberately provoked limited engagements and then executed preplanned tactics to evaluate the response, the principle has virtually unlimited applicability.

7

Military Combat

In general, the strategy for employing the army is this: From the time the general receives his commands from the ruler, unites the armies, and assembles the masses to confronting the enemy and encamping, there is nothing more difficult than military combat. In military combat what is most difficult is turning the circuitous into the straight, turning adversity into advantage.

Thus if you make the enemy's path circuitous and entice them with profit, although you set out after them you will arrive before them. This results from knowing the tactics of the circuitous and the direct.

Combat between armies is advantageous, combat between masses is dangerous. You will not arrive in time if the entire army contends for advantage. But if you reduce the army's size to contend for advantage, your baggage and heavy equipment will suffer losses.

For this reason, if you abandon your armor and heavy equipment to race forward day and night without encamping, covering two days' normal distance at a time, marching forward a hundred *li* to contend for gain, the Three Armies' generals will be captured. The strong will be first to arrive, the exhausted will follow. With such tactics only one in ten will reach the battle site.

If you contend for gain fifty *li* away, it will cause the general of the Upper Army to stumble, and by following such tactics half the men will reach the objective. If you contend for gain at thirty *li*, then two thirds of the army will reach the objective.

Accordingly, if the army does not have baggage and heavy equipment it will be lost; if it does not have provisions it will be lost; if it does not have stores it will be lost.

Those who do not know the plans of the feudal lords cannot prepare alliances beforehand. Those unfamiliar with the mountains and forests, the gorges and defiles, the shape of marshes and wetlands cannot advance the army. Those who do not employ local guides cannot gain advantages of terrain.

The army is established by deceit, moves for advantage, and changes through segmenting and reuniting. Thus its speed is like the wind, its slowness like the forest. Its invasion and plundering are like fire. Unmoving, it is like the mountains. It is as difficult to know as the darkness; in movement it is like thunder.

Divide the wealth among your troops when you plunder a district. Divide the profits when you enlarge your territory.

Take control of the strategic balance of power and move. Those who first understand the tactics of the circuitous and the direct will be victorious. This is the strategy for military combat.

The *Military Administration* states: "Because they could not hear each other they made gongs and drums; because they could not see each other they made pennants and flags."

Gongs, drums, pennants, and flags are the means to unify the men's ears and eyes. When the men have been unified, the courageous will not be able to advance alone, the fearful will not be able to retreat alone. This is the method for employing large numbers.

Thus, in night battles make the fires and drums numerous, and in daylight battles make the flags and pennants numerous in order to change the men's ears and eyes.

The *ch'i* (*qi*) of the Three Armies can be snatched away; the commanding general's mind can be seized. For this reason in the morning their *ch'i* is ardent; during the day their *ch'i* becomes indolent; at dusk their *ch'i* is exhausted. Therefore, one who excels at employing the army avoids their ardent *ch'i* and strikes when it is indolent or exhausted. This is the way to manipulate *ch'i*.

In order await the disordered, in tranquility await the clamorous. This is the way to control the mind.

With the near await the distant; with the rested await the fatigued; with the sated await the hungry. This is the way to control strength.

Do not intercept well-ordered flags, do not attack well-regulated formations. This is the way to control change.

Thus the strategy for employing the military:

> Do not approach high mountains.
> Do not confront those who have hills behind them.
> Do not pursue feigned retreats.
> Do not attack animated troops.
> Do not swallow an army acting as bait.
> Do not obstruct an army retreating homeward.

If you besiege an army, you must leave an outlet.
Do not press an exhausted invader.
These are the strategies for employing the military.

o o o

Although titled "Military Combat," the chapter focuses upon the preliminaries to battle, unfolding operational principles, and methods of control designed to maximize one's own strength and readiness while simultaneously enervating and debilitating the enemy. The concept of *ch'i* (*qi*)—the "spirit," morale, or dedication of the troops—underlies virtually all the pronouncements. Moreover, nurturing and manipulating *ch'i*, a core psychological topic in all the Chinese military writings, is initiated by the chapter's famous description of the three battlefield phases.

The late Warring States *Wei Liao-tzu* (*Wei Liaozi*) summarized *ch'i's* vital importance: "The means by which the people fight is their *ch'i*. When their *ch'i* is substantial they will fight; when their *ch'i* has been snatched away they will run off." Accordingly, Sun-tzu counseled that "one who excels at employing the army avoids their ardent *ch'i* and strikes when it is indolent or exhausted." But because events would not usually be so simply or fortuitously structured, measures to exhaust an opponent's *ch'i* must be actively pursued.

Because physical condition provides the essential foundation for the soldier's morale, making the enemy's movement more arduous invariably affects their enthusiasm. Hunger will further weaken them, and providing an escape will psychologically undermine their commitment in difficult situations as well as preclude the surge of fervent spirit often elicited by hopeless circumstances.

Conversely, while implementing the necessary measures for discipline and control, perspicacious commanders will conserve the army's energy and ensure that their troops are in peak condition when they await the enemy. This is accomplished by eschewing the overly rapid and disorganized advances that can turn the most cohesive force into a disorganized rabble; by astute prepositioning; and by avoiding the hundred illnesses that always plague expeditionary troops. Unstated, but equally important, their own spirits must be nurtured so that at the time of the engagement they comprise a single motivated force that can easily overwhelm the enemy's dispirited hordes.

Like most chapters in the *Art of War*, "Military Combat" also encompasses various discrete pronouncements on essential matters, frequently reiterations of principles previously raised or upcoming focal subjects, such as deceit and intelligence. It concludes with eight concrete operational admonitions that no doubt reflect the era's common military wisdom and practices, such as not confronting those who have hills behind them. Particularly important is the warning not to be enticed by apparent retreats and isolated forces into overly committing and thereby exposing one's troops, the feigned retreat being a well-developed ancient Chinese technique.

九
変

8

Nine Changes

In general, after the general has received his commands from the ruler, united the armies, and assembled the masses, the strategy for employing the military is:

Do not encamp on entrapping terrain.

Unite with your allies on focal terrain.

Do not remain on isolated terrain.

Make strategic plans for encircled terrain.

You must do battle on fatal terrain.

There are roads that are not followed.

There are armies that are not attacked.

There are fortified cities that are not assaulted.

There is terrain for which one does not contend.

There are commands from the ruler that are not accepted.

As for the "roads that are not followed": When we enter enemy territory shallowly, affairs to the fore will not be known. When we enter deeply, advantages to the rear cannot be consolidated. If we move it will not be advantageous, but if we remain still we will be imprisoned. In such cases do not follow them.

As for "armies that are not attacked": Our two armies have intercepted each other and encamped. We estimate that our strength is sufficient to destroy their army and capture their generals. However, assessing it from a long-range perspective, there are those who excel in unorthodox strategic power and skillful tactics among them, and their army is well ordered. In such cases, even though their army can be attacked, do not attack it.

As for "fortified cities that are not assaulted": We estimate that our strength is sufficient to seize a city. However, if we seize it, it will not be of any advantage to the fore, but if we gain it, we will not be able to protect it to the rear. If our strength equals theirs, the city certainly will not be taken. If, when we gain the advantages of a forward position, the city will then surrender by itself, and if we do not gain such advantages the city will not cause harm to the rear, even though the city can be assaulted, do not assault it.

As for "terrain that is not contested": Do not contend for the terrain in mountain valleys where the water is unable to sustain life.

As for "orders of the ruler that are not implemented": If the ruler's orders contravene these four changes, do not implement them. One who truly understands these changes in affairs knows how to employ the military.

Generals who have a penetrating understanding of the advantages of the nine changes know how to employ the army. Generals who do not have a penetrating understanding of the advantages of the nine changes, even though they may be familiar with the topography, will not be able to realize the advantages of terrain.

Even if they are familiar with the five advantages, anyone who commands an army but does not know the techniques for the nine changes will not be able to control men.

For this reason the wise must contemplate the intermixture of gain and loss. Their efforts can be trusted if they discern advantage in difficult situations. Difficulties can be resolved if they discern harm in prospective advantage.

Accordingly, subjugate the feudal lords with potential harm; labor the feudal lords with numerous affairs; and have the feudal lords race after profits.

The strategy for employing the army: Do not rely on their not coming, but depend upon having the means to await them. Do not rely on their not attacking, but depend upon having an unassailable position.

Generals have five dangerous character traits:

>   Those committed to dying can be slain.

>   Those committed to living can be captured.

>   Those easily angered and hasty to act can be insulted.

>   Those obsessed with being scrupulous and untainted can be shamed.

>   Those who love the people can be troubled.

Now these five dangerous traits are excesses in a general, potential disaster for employing the army. The army's destruction and the general's death will invariably stem from these five, so they must be investigated.

○   ○   ○

The chapter commences by identifying inimical situations that should be avoided and objectives that must not be assaulted, the former because the terrain's configuration hinders essential movement, the latter because the army may easily be defeated or become entangled. (Configuration of terrain being a crucial organizing concept in early Chinese military science, these five terrains recur in later chapters where they receive further explication. But their defining characteristics are readily apparent from their names, therefore the need for further definition is obviated.)

Knowledge of the topography, gained through local informants and reconnaissance, is critical to formulating operational tactics and deploying the army. Furthermore, insofar as every situation encompasses potential advantage and disadvantage, the general must "contemplate the intermixture of gain and loss" and carefully assess the possibility of achieving his objectives before engaging the enemy. (Even Mao Tse-tung employed Sun-tzu's view when he stressed the need to discern and exploit the possible advantages entailed by difficult strategic situations.) In addition, mounting a strong, preemptive defense and thorough preparation are recommended to preclude the army's becoming vulnerable to unexpected attacks or being helplessly caught in straitened circumstances.

The general being synonymous with the army's fate, the final section enumerates several command flaws that can easily doom it to defeat, whether as a result of self-generated errors or through perspicacious enemies who deliberately exploit the flaws. Intensive intelligence efforts and active battlefield probing were devoted to detecting weaknesses in enemy commanders. Perhaps because of their inclusion in the *Art of War*, over the centuries among the most prominent were the polarized pair of being too committed to living and thus afraid of dying, and of being committed to dying gloriously to achieve a lasting reputation. On the battlefield the former prove too timid, the latter too rash, particularly if the commanders are headstrong and courageous. However, commanders must be sufficiently confident and unconcerned with reputation to ignore dangerous imperial directives.

Among the other potentially exploitable and assuredly detrimental traits found throughout the text, perhaps the most initially perplexing is that "one who loves the people can be troubled." However, clearly Sun-tzu wanted to warn against commanders who were too cautious to exercise aggressive command or too fearful of losses to undertake reasonable risks. Instead of quickly wresting victory by judiciously expending their troops for the greater good of the state, they ineffectually deploy their forces and suffer debilitating defeats, frequently through a loss of initiative and *ch'i*. The benevolent practice of warfare paradoxically requires ruthlessness and resoluteness.

行
軍 *9*

Maneuvering the Army

As for deploying the army and fathoming the enemy:

To cross mountains, follow the valleys, search out tenable ground, and occupy the heights. If the enemy holds the heights, do not climb up to engage them in battle. This is the way to deploy an army in the mountains.

After crossing rivers you must distance yourself from them. If the enemy is fording a river to advance, do not confront them in the water. It will be advantageous to strike them when half their forces have crossed.

If you want to engage the enemy in battle, do not array your forces near the river to confront the invader but look for tenable ground and occupy the heights. Do not confront the current's flow. This is the way to deploy the army where there are rivers.

When you cross salt marshes and wetlands, concentrate on quickly getting away from them, do not remain. If you engage in battle in marshes or wet-lands, you must stay in areas with marsh grass and keep groves of trees at your back. This is the way to deploy the army in marshes and wetlands.

On level plains deploy on easy terrain so that the right flank is positioned with high ground to the rear, fatal terrain to the fore, and tenable terrain to the rear. This is the way to deploy on the plains.

These four deployments, advantageous to the army, are the means by which the Yellow Emperor conquered the four emperors.

Now the army likes heights and abhors low areas, es-teems *yang* (the sunny) and disdains *yin* (the shady). It nourishes life and occupies the substantial. An army that avoids the hundred illnesses is said to be certain of victory.

Where there are hills and embankments you must occupy the *yang* side, keeping them to the right rear. This is to the army's advantage and exploits the natu-ral assistance of the terrain.

Foam appears when it rains upstream. Wait until it settles if you want to cross over.

You must quickly get away from deadly configurations of terrain such as precipitous gorges with mountain torrents, Heaven's Well, Heaven's Jail, Heaven's Net, Heaven's Pit, and Heaven's Fissure.

Do not approach them. When we keep them at a distance, the enemy is forced to approach them. When we face them, the enemy is compelled to have them at their rear.

When the army encounters ravines and defiles, wetlands with reeds and tall grass, mountain forests, or areas with heavy, entangled undergrowth on the flanks, you must thoroughly search them because they are places where an ambush or spies will be concealed.

If an enemy in close proximity remains quiet, they are relying on their tactical occupation of ravines.

If they challenge you to battle while far off, they want you to advance because they occupy easy terrain to their advantage.

If large numbers of trees move, they are approaching.

If there are many visible obstacles in the heavy grass, it is to make us suspicious.

If birds take flight, there is an ambush.

If the animals are afraid, enemy forces are mounting a sudden attack.

If dust rises high up in a sharply defined column, chariots are coming. If it is low and broad, the infantry is advancing. If it disperses into thin shafts, they are gathering firewood. If it is sparse, coming and going, they are encamping.

Those who speak deferentially but increase their preparations will advance.

Those who speak belligerently and hastily advance will retreat.

Those whose light chariots first fan out to the sides are deploying for battle.

Those who seek peace without setting any prior conditions are executing a stratagem.

Those whose troops race off but they then deploy their armies into formation are implementing a predetermined schedule.

Those whose troops half advance and half retreat are enticing you.

Those who stand about leaning on their weapons are hungry.

When those who draw water drink first, they are thirsty.

Those who see potential gain but do not know whether to advance are tired.

Where birds congregate it is empty.

If the enemy cries out at night, they are afraid.

If the army is turbulent, their general lacks severity.

If their flags and pennants move about, they are in chaos.

If their officers are angry, they are exhausted.

If they kill their horses and eat the meat, the army lacks grain.

If they hang up their cooking utensils and do not return to camp, they are an exhausted invader.

Those whose troops repeatedly congregate in small groups here and there, whispering together, have lost the masses.

Those who frequently grant rewards are in deep distress.

Those who frequently impose punishments are in great difficulty.

Those who are at first excessively brutal and then fear the masses are the pinnacle of stupidity.

Those who have emissaries come forth with offerings want to rest for a while.

You must carefully investigate it if their troops are aroused and approach our forces only to maintain their positions without engaging in battle or breaking off the confrontation.

The army does not esteem the number of troops being more numerous for it only means you cannot aggressively advance. It is sufficient for you to muster your own strength, analyze the enemy, and take them. Only those who lack strategic planning and slight their enemies will inevitably be captured by others.

If you impose punishments on the troops before they have become attached, they will not be submissive. If they are not submissive, they will be difficult to employ. If you do not impose punishments after the troops have become attached, they cannot be used.

Thus, commanding them with the civil and unifying them through the martial is referred to as "being certain to take them."

If orders are consistently implemented to instruct the people, the people will submit. If orders are not consistently implemented to instruct the people, the people will not submit. Those whose orders are consistently carried out have established a mutual relationship with the people.

o   o   o

Much of "Maneuvering the Army" warns against troublesome terrain where ambushes may be concealed, mobility hampered, freedom of maneuver denied, and forces entrapped and slaughtered. Conversely, the army should concentrate upon exploiting easy ground and encamping on land that will sustain life while taking advantage of difficult and constrained configurations by forcing the enemy onto them, dominating the heights, and exploiting the resulting imbalance with overwhelming strategic power. (Presumably because the *Art of War*'s authors were active in the Jiangsu region, where the theory and practice of chariot-based, plains warfare were ineffectual, rivers and wetlands receive singular attention.)

Although the chief characteristics of these fatal terrains are well imagized by their names, Heaven's Pit has traditionally been understood as an enclosed area marked by soft, muddy ground. Heaven's Fissure reputedly encompasses long, narrow passages constrained by hills or forests; Heaven's Well is probably a significant depression that can be inundated by an unexpected runoff of rainwater; Heaven's Jail delimits a valley with steep hills or mountains on three sides; and Heaven's Net refers to areas of extensive, dense growth that will obstruct the passage of vehicles or entangle men.

In concord with the fundamental assumptions that warfare has to be conducted on a rational basis and that the enemy can be fathomed, the chapter identifies several commonly witnessed behaviors before correlating them with strategy and intent and thereby initiating a continuous evaluative tradition. (These and other techniques for penetrating enemy behavior are extensively discussed in our *Tao of Spycraft: Intelligence Theory and Practice in Traditional China.*) Of particular importance is the admonition to beware of peace proposals because they may conceal a desire to rest and regroup, the ensuing interval as well as prospects for the conflict's cessation undermining determination, spirit, and awareness.

The assertion that troop strength does not constitute the sole determinant of a battle's outcome is somewhat surprising given previous admonitions to adopt a defensive stance when outnumbered, but it reflects the *Art of War*'s emphasis upon manipulating the enemy and Sun-tzu's confidence in the efficacy of maneuver warfare. However, stringent yet balanced measures for command and control must be adopted to enable any form of field combat whatsoever. Three critical issues require pondering: the need to nurture the troops' emotional allegiance before applying punishments; the need to adopt civil and martial measures systematically, the former encompassing virtue, deference, beneficence, and rewards, the latter entailing directness, energy, strict commands, and punishments; and the need to ensure trust in the orders and confidence in the commander's actions.

地
形 **10**
Configurations of Terrain

The major configurations of terrain are accessible, suspended, stalemated, constricted, precipitous, and expansive.

If you can go forth and the enemy can also advance, it is termed "accessible." First occupy the heights and *yang* side in accessible configurations, and improve the transport routes for provisions. Then it will prove advantageous to engage in battle.

If you can go forth but it will be difficult to return, it is termed "suspended." Go forth and conquer them on suspended configurations if they are unprepared. But if the enemy is prepared and you sally forth without being victorious, it will be difficult to turn back and will not be advantageous.

If it is not advantageous for you to go forth nor advantageous for the enemy to come forward, it is termed "stalemated." Do not go forth in a stalemated configuration even though the enemy tries to entice you with profit. Withdraw your forces and depart. But if you can then strike them when half the enemy has come forth, it will be advantageous.

If you are the first to occupy a constricted configuration, you must fully deploy throughout it in order to await the enemy. If the enemy occupies it first and fully deploys, do not follow them in. However, if they do not fully deploy, then follow them in.

If you occupy a precipitous configuration, you must hold the heights and *yang* sides to await the enemy. If the enemy occupies it first, withdraw your forces and depart. Do not follow them.

If your strategic power is equal, it will be difficult to provoke the enemy into combat on an expansive configuration. Engaging in combat would not be advantageous.

Now these six are the Tao of terrain. Every general undertaking responsibility for command must investigate them.

There are six types of ill-fated armies: running off, lax, sinking, crumbling, chaotic, and routed. Now these six are not disasters brought about by Heaven and Earth, but by the commanding general's errors.

Now if one attacks ten despite their strategic power being equal, this is called "running off."

If the troops are strong but the officers weak, it is termed "lax."

If the officers are strong but the troops weak, it is termed "sinking."

If the higher officers insubordinately engage the enemy out of unrestrained anger before the general even knows their capability, it is termed "crumbling."

If the general is weak and not strict, unenlightened in his instructions and leadership; the officers and troops lack constant duties; and their deployment of troops into formation is askew, it is termed "chaotic."

If the general, unable to fathom the enemy, engages a large number with a small number or attacks the strong with the weak while the army lacks a properly selected vanguard, it is termed "routed."

Now these six are the Tao of defeat. Any general who undertakes responsibility for command must investigate them.

Configuration of terrain is an aid to the army. Analyzing the enemy, taking control of victory, estimating ravines and defiles, the distant and near, is the Tao of the superior general. Anyone who knows them and employs them in combat will certainly be victorious, anyone who does not know them or employ them in combat will certainly be defeated.

If the Tao of Warfare indicates certain victory, even though the ruler has instructed that combat should be avoided, if you must engage in battle it is permissible. If the Tao of Warfare indicates you will not be victorious, even though the ruler instructs you to engage in battle, not fighting is permissible.

The general who does not advance to seek fame or fail to retreat to avoid being charged with the capital offense of retreating, but seeks only to preserve the people and gain advantage for the ruler is the state's treasure.

When the general regards his troops as young children, they will advance into the deepest valleys with him. When he regards the troops as his beloved children, they will be willing to die with him.

If they are well treated but cannot be employed, if they are loved but cannot be commanded, or when in chaos they cannot be governed, they may be compared to arrogant children and cannot be used.

Knowing that our troops can attack but not knowing the enemy cannot be attacked is only halfway to victory. Knowing that the enemy can be attacked but not realizing our troops cannot attack is only halfway to victory. Knowing that the enemy can be attacked and that our army can effect the attack, but not knowing the terrain is not suitable for combat, is only halfway to victory. Thus one who truly knows the army will never be deluded when he moves, never be impoverished when initiating an action.

Thus it is said if you know them and know yourself, your victory will not be imperiled. If you know Heaven and know Earth, your victory can be complete.

o   o   o

Although ostensibly focused on the core concept of configurations of terrain, the chapter also contains important, though rarely cited, material about command and control. But not content simply to describe problematic imbalances in authority and effort and chart their effects on battlefield performance, "Configurations of Terrain" also boldly reasserts the field commander's necessary independence regardless of imperial directives. Nevertheless, this independence presumes surpassing competence in the commander as well as a sound foundation in intelligence and assessment practices. The chapter therefore concludes with an astonishingly well-known paragraph, similar to the one articulated at the end of "Planning Offensives," that reiterates not just the inescapable need to know the enemy and oneself but also the entire situation, the patterns of Heaven and Earth. (Having vanished from common language, the second part—"If you know Heaven and know Earth, your victory can be complete"—is rarely cited in broader contexts today.)

"Configurations of Terrain" is the first of two consecutive chapters that strategically assess a wide range of generalized, recurring topographical features by correlating the operational impact of their characteristics with appropriate tactical measures. It thus comprises a partial, analytic realization of the *Art of War*'s initial thrust—"Earth encompasses high or low, far or near, difficult or easy, expansive or confined ground, fatal or tenable terrain"—and the principle "Configuration of terrain is an aid to the army. Analyzing the enemy, taking control of victory, estimating ravines and defiles, the distant and near, is the Tao of the superior general."

Although the categories are a crucial organizing topic for which generalized discussion is best deferred to the Afterword, they perhaps merit a few comments here despite the presumably descriptive names chosen to translate the respective terms. However, it is assumed that two significant forces are confronting each other, each fully capable of combat and maneuver except as the situation may constrain them. Accessible terrain then refers not just to unbounded plains—topography more properly entailed by "expansive terrain"—or ground lacking significant barriers or impediments, but rather to areas accessible to troops arriving from any direction.

Armies finding themselves confronting "suspended" terrain, being unable to recover their initial position, will be stymied if they advance, and thus hung up or suspended. Conversely, on "stalemated" terrain, both sides are well supported; neither side is able to wrest a significant advantage from the ground and a lengthy standoff is likely. Accordingly, withdrawing might entice the enemy into advancing, making them vulnerable to attack once in motion and destabilized. "Precipitous" terrain, a broad category that also embraces such killing grounds as Heaven's Pit, invokes the image of sharp ravines and steep mountain gorges, tortuously difficult and dangerous to traverse.

九地

11

Nine Terrains

The strategy for employing the military is this: There is dispersive terrain, light terrain, contentious terrain, traversable terrain, focal terrain, heavy terrain, entrapping terrain, encircled terrain, and fatal terrain.

When the feudal lords fight in their own territory, it is "dispersive" terrain. Do not engage the enemy on dispersive terrain.

When they enter someone else's territory, but not deeply, it is "light terrain." Do not stop on light terrain.

If, when you occupy it, it will be advantageous to you, but if they occupy it, it will be advantageous to them, it is "contentious" terrain. Do not attack on contentious terrain.

When you can go forth and they can also come forward, it is "traversable" (accessible) terrain. Do not allow your forces to become isolated on traversable terrain.

Land of the feudal lords surrounded on three sides such that whoever arrives first will gain the masses of All under Heaven is "focal" terrain. Unite and form alliances with nearby feudal lords on focal terrain.

When you penetrate deeply into enemy territory, bypassing numerous cities, it is "heavy" terrain. Plunder for provisions on heavy terrain.

Where there are mountains and forests, ravines and defiles, wetlands and marshes, wherever the road is difficult to negotiate, it is "entrapping" terrain. Move quickly through entrapping terrain.

Where the entrance is constricted, the return is circuitous, and with a small number they can strike your masses, it is "encircled" terrain. Use strategy on encircled terrain.

Where if you fight with intensity you will survive, but if you do not fight with intensity you will perish, it is "fatal" terrain. Engage in battle on fatal terrain.

In antiquity, those who were referred to as excelling in the employment of the army were able to keep the enemy's forward and rear forces from connecting; the many and few from relying on each other; the noble and lowly from coming to each other's rescue; the upper and lower ranks from trusting each other; and the troops separated, unable to reassemble, or when assembled, not well-ordered. They moved when it was advantageous, halted when it was not advantageous.

If I dare ask, if the enemy is numerous, disciplined, and about to advance, how should we respond to them? I would say, first seize something that they love for then they will listen to you.

It is the nature of the army to stress speed; to take advantage of the enemy's absence; to travel unanticipated roads; and to attack when they are not alert.

In general, the Tao of an invader is that the army will be unified when you have penetrated deeply into enemy territory and the defenders will not be able to conquer you.

If you forage in the fertile countryside, then the Three Armies will have enough to eat. If you carefully nurture them and do not over-labor them, their *ch'i* (*qi*) will be united and their strength will be at maximum.

You must be unfathomable when you mobilize the army and form strategic plans.

Cast them into positions from which there is nowhere to go and they will die without retreating. If there is no escape from death, the officers and soldiers will fully exhaust their strength.

When the soldiers and officers have penetrated deeply into enemy territory, they will cling together. When there is no alternative, they will fight.

For this reason, even though the soldiers are not instructed, they are prepared; without seeking it, their cooperation is obtained; without covenants, they are close together; without issuing orders, they are reliable. Prohibit omens, eliminate doubt so that they will die without other thoughts.

If our soldiers do not have excessive wealth, it is not because they detest material goods. If they do not live long lives, it is not because they abhor longevity. On the day that the orders are issued the tears of the soldiers who are sitting will soak their sleeves, while the tears of those lying down will roll down their cheeks. However, if you throw them into a hopeless situation, they will have the courage of *Chu (Zhu)* or *Kuei (Gui)*.

Thus anyone who excels at employing the army may be compared to the snake known as the *shuaijan*. The *shuaijan (shuairan)* is found on Mount Ch'ang. If you strike its head, the tail will respond; if you strike its tail, the head will respond. If you strike the middle, both the head and tail will react.

If I dare ask, can we make the army like the *shuaijan*, I would say that we can. For example, the people of

Wu and Yüeh hate each other, but if they encounter severe wind when fording a river in the same boat, their efforts to rescue each other will be like the left and right hands.

For this reason, fettering the horses and burying the chariot wheels are inadequate measures for preventing the soldiers from fleeing. Unify their courage to be as one through the Tao of administration. Realize the appropriate employment of the hard and soft through the patterns of terrain.

Thus one who excels at employing the army leads them by the hand as if they were only one man, so they cannot avoid it.

It is essential for a general to be tranquil and obscure, upright and self-disciplined, and able to stupefy the eyes and ears of the officers and troops, keeping them ignorant. He alters his management of affairs and changes his strategies to keep other people from recognizing them. He shifts his position and traverses indirect routes to keep other people from being able to anticipate him.

At the moment the general has designated with them, it will be as if they ascended a height and abandoned their ladders. The general advances with them deep into the territory of the feudal lords and then releases the trigger. He commands them as if racing a herd of sheep—they are driven away, driven back, but no one knows where they are going.

Assembling the masses of the Three Armies and casting them into danger are the general's responsibility.

The nine transformations of terrain—the advantages deriving from contraction and expansion, the patterns of human emotions—must be investigated.

In general, the Tao of the invader is this:

When the troops have penetrated deeply they will be unified, but where only shallowly, they will be inclined to scatter.

When the army has left the state, crossed the enemy's border, and is on campaign, it is "isolated" terrain.

When the four sides are open, it is "focal" terrain.

When you have advanced deeply, it is "heavy" terrain.

If you have penetrated only shallowly, it is "light" terrain.

If you have strongholds behind you and constrictions before you, it is "encircled" terrain.

If there is no place to go, it is "fatal" terrain.

Accordingly, on dispersive terrain I unify their will.

On light terrain I have them group together.

On contentious terrain I race our rear elements forward.

On traversable terrain I focus on defense.

On focal terrain I solidify our alliances.

On heavy terrain I ensure a continuous supply of provisions.

On entrapping terrain I speedily advance along the roads.

On encircled terrain I obstruct any openings.

On fatal terrain I show them that we will not live.

Thus it is the nature of the army to defend when encircled; to fight fervently when unavoidable; and to follow orders when compelled by circumstances.

For this reason those who do not know the plans of the feudal lords cannot forge preparatory alliances. Those who do not know the topography of mountains and forests, ravines and defiles, wetlands and marshes cannot maneuver the army. Those who do not employ local guides will not secure advantages of terrain. Those who do not know even one of these four or five cannot command the army of a hegemon or a true king.

Now when the army of a hegemon or true king attacks a great state, their masses are unable to assemble. When it applies its awesomeness to the enemy, their alliances cannot be sustained. For this reason it does not contend with any alliances under Heaven. It does not nurture the authority of others under Heaven. Have faith in yourself, apply your awesomeness to the enemy. Then their cities can be taken, their state can be subjugated.

Bestow rewards not required by law, impose exceptional governmental orders. Direct the masses of the Three Armies as though commanding one man. Press affairs upon them, do not explain the purpose to them. Compel them with prospects for profit, but do not inform them about the potential harm.

Cast them into hopeless situations and they will be preserved; have them penetrate fatal terrain and they will live. Only after the masses have penetrated dangerous terrain will they be able to craft victory out of defeat.

The prosecution of military affairs lies in (learning in detail) and according with the enemy's intentions. Anyone who then focuses his strength toward the enemy, strikes a thousand *li* away, and kills their general is termed "skillful and capable in completing military affairs."

On the day the government mobilizes the army close the passes, destroy all tallies, and do not allow their emissaries to pass through. Hold intense strategic discussions in the upper hall of the temple in order to bring about the execution of affairs.

If the enemy opens the door, you must race in.

Attack what they love first. Do not fix any time for battle, assess and react to the enemy in order to determine the strategy for battle.

For this reason at first be like a virgin (at home); later, when the enemy opens the door, be like a fleeing rabbit. The enemy will be unable to withstand you.

o   o   o

The *Art of War*'s longest chapter, "Nine Terrains," reiterates several crucial, loosely integrated principles as part of its continuing examination of topographical implications. Aggressive measures based upon sound knowledge should be actively implemented to balk the enemy's alliances, frustrate their plans, and destroy their cohesion, rendering them ineffective and vulnerable. Primary among them is creating and preserving the commander's unfathomability, whether to the enemy or to his own troops, thereby causing sufficient uncertainty to prevent attacks from being anticipated or preemptive defenses mounted. Whenever combat with large, disciplined forces becomes inevitable, coercive leverage can be gained by "first seizing something that they love."

Although the title specifies nine terrains, several more appear because the chapter contains two separate enumerations. Some of the terms overlap each other and previous definitions; others, though never fully contradictory, vary. Over the centuries, commentators have striven to reconcile apparent differences by concocting numerous clever but tortuous explanations. However, it should be recalled that these laconic statements were originally oral pronouncements, more core summaries for teaching and remembering; indeed, their extemporaneous nature virtually assured that different versions would coexist when subsequently gathered and loosely systematized. Nevertheless, the vision remains the same: "The nine transformations of terrain must be investigated" and "One who does not know the topography of mountains and forests, ravines and defiles, wetlands and marshes cannot maneuver the army."

Because it ponders the various configurations of terrain and their correlated tactical constraints for an expeditionary force advancing from their own borders onto enemy territory, however, the discussion is marked by a different orientation. It not only falls within, but also essentially initiates the psychological analysis of martial mental and behavioral states that would subsequently be expanded in Sun Pin's *Military Methods* and similar works.

Troop cohesion and battlefield commitment were seen as increasing in tandem with the invasion's penetration of enemy territory, the greatest courage being witnessed on "fatal" terrain: "When the soldiers and officers have penetrated deeply into enemy territory, they will cling together. When there is no alternative, they will fight." Conversely, because such desperate fervency is frequently required to wrest victory, it can be artificially summoned by deliberately thrusting the troops into "fatal" situations: "Cast them into positions from which there is nowhere to go and they will die without retreating. If there is no escape from death, the officers and soldiers will fully exhaust their strength." However, effective command and control measures must be implemented throughout, and all contrary stimuli that might undermine their resoluteness, such as omens, excluded.

12

Incendiary Attack

There are five types of incendiary attack: The first is to incinerate men, the second to incinerate provisions, the third to incinerate supply trains, the fourth to incinerate armories, and the fifth to incinerate formations.

Implementing an incendiary attack depends on the proper conditions. Equipment for incendiary attack should be fully prepared before required. Launching an incendiary attack has its appropriate seasons, igniting the fire the proper days.

As for the seasons, it is the time of the dry spell; as for the day, when the moon is in *chi (ji)*, *pi (bi)*, *yi*, or *chen (zhen)*. Wind will arise on the days when it is in these four lunar lodges.

In general, in incendiary warfare you must respond to the five changes of fire:

If fires are started within their camp, then you should immediately respond with an attack from outside.

If fires are ignited but their army remains quiet, then wait, do not attack.

When they flare into a conflagration, if you can follow up, then do so; if you cannot, then desist.

If the attack can be launched from outside without relying on inside assistance, initiate it at an appropriate time.

If fires are ignited upwind, do not attack downwind. Winds that arise in the daytime will persist, those that arise at night will stop.

Now the army must know the five changes of fire in order to defend against them at the astrologically appropriate times. Thus using fire to aid an attack is enlightened, using water to assist an attack is powerful. Water can be used to sever, but cannot be employed to seize.

Now if someone is victorious in battle and succeeds in attack but does not exploit the achievement, it is disastrous and his fate should be termed "wasteful and tarrying." Thus it is said the wise general ponders it, the good general cultivates it.

If it is not advantageous, do not move. If objectives cannot be attained, do not employ the army. Unless endangered do not engage in warfare.

The ruler cannot mobilize the army out of personal anger. The general cannot engage in battle because of personal frustration. When it is advantageous, move; when not advantageous, stop. Anger can revert to happiness, annoyance can revert to joy, but a vanquished state cannot be revived, the dead cannot be brought back to life.

Thus the enlightened ruler is cautious about it, the good general respectful of it. This is the Tao for bringing security to the state and preserving the army intact.

o   o   o

As early as the Neolithic period fire was occasionally employed in China to facilitate attacks on walled towns and to destroy vanquished enemies; however, incendiary techniques did not become an essential tactical component until fortified cities began to suffer lengthy sieges and encampments were increasingly targeted for massive assaults during the spring and autumn. "Incendiary Attack" reflects these developments and constitutes the first known theoretical articulation of incendiary warfare. Despite the subsequent ingenious developments in methods, materials, and tactics, which are described in our book on traditional incendiary and aquatic warfare in China, *Fire and Water*, "Incendiary Attack" continued to furnish the basis for virtually all later contemplations of the subject, its principles and observations generally being cited intact.

Because arrows, stones, and other projectiles are all instantaneously expended, fire and water were the only forces before the evolution of gunpowder-based explosives that had an impact beyond the moment of action. Fire can not only spread and grow once unleashed, its terrifying power can disrupt the most disciplined of forces and well-organized cities even when not inflicting great damage. Although the flames can also inflict casualties—particularly if troops are directly targeted—they historically had a greater effect in depriving the enemy of the materials and provisions necessary to sustain their campaigns, maintain defenses, and wage war.

By concluding with a strong admonition against squandering hard-won battlefield achievements and an equally forceful enjoinder not to recklessly engage in warfare because of momentary anger or other emotional impulses, the second part of the chapter essentially returns to the theme of "Initial Estimations." Although "Incendiary Attack" would therefore seem to depart radically from the topic of incendiary warfare, fire was primarily conceived and employed as preparing the ground for further gains and action rather than simply destruction for its own sake. Within the context of Sun-tzu's emphasis upon achieving victory at the least possible cost—the ruthless practice of efficient warfare—any failure to exploit a localized victory could only be condemned, a point equally emphasized in Mao Tse-tung's military writings.

Although this injunction was well known, whether out of fear of failure or overconfidence in their achievements, many Chinese generals proved timid in subsequent centuries, thereby allowing the enemy to regroup and sometimes reverse almost inevitable results. No doubt the danger of erroneously assessing the situation and the frequent successes of ruses and feigned surrenders constituted mental obstacles that robbed apparently resolute commanders of their will and so deprived the state of victory.

用
間

13

Employing Spies

When you send an army of a hundred thousand forth on a campaign, marching them out a thousand *li*, the expenditures of the common people and the contributions of the feudal house will be one thousand pieces of gold per day. Those inconvenienced and troubled both within and without the border, who are exhausted on the road or unable to pursue their agricultural work, will be seven hundred thousand families.

Armies remain locked in a standoff for years to fight for victory on a single day, yet generals begrudge bestowing ranks and emoluments of one hundred pieces of gold and therefore do not know the enemy's situation. This is the ultimate inhumanity. Such a person is not a general for the people, an assistant for the ruler, or the arbiter of victory.

The means by which enlightened rulers and sagacious generals moved and conquered others, that their achievements surpassed the masses, was advance knowledge.

Advance knowledge cannot be gained from ghosts and spirits, inferred from phenomena, or projected from the measures of Heaven, but must be gained from men for it is the knowledge of the enemy's true situation.

Thus there are five types of spies to be employed: local spy, internal spy, turned spy (double agent), dead (expendable) spy, and the living spy. When all five are employed together and no one knows the Tao of their employment, it is termed "spiritual methodology." They are a ruler's treasures.

Local spies—employ people from the local district.

Internal spies—employ their officials.

Double agents—employ the enemy's spies.

Expendable spies—employ them to spread disinformation outside the state. Provide our expendable spies with false information and have them leak it to enemy agents.

Living spies—return with their reports.

Thus of all the Three Armies' affairs no relationship is closer than with spies; no rewards are more generous than those given to spies; no affairs are more secret than those pertaining to spies.

Unless someone has the wisdom of a Sage, he cannot use spies; unless he is benevolent and righteous, he cannot employ spies; unless he is subtle and perspicacious, he cannot perceive the substance in intelligence reports. It is subtle, subtle! There are no areas in which one does not employ spies.

If the mission is exposed before it has begun, the spy and all those he informed should be put to death.

In general, as for the armies you want to strike, the cities you want to attack, and the men you want to assassinate, you must first know the names of the defensive commander, his assistants, staff, door guards, and attendants. You must have your spies search out and learn them all.

You must search for enemy agents who have come to spy on us. Tempt them with profits, instruct and retain them, thereby obtaining and employing double agents. Through knowledge gained from them you can recruit both local and internal spies. Through knowledge gained from them the expendable spy can spread his falsehoods and be used to misinform the enemy. Through knowledge gained from them our living spies can be employed as the moment requires.

The ruler must know these five aspects of espionage work. Because such knowledge invariably depends on turned spies, you must be generous to double agents.

In antiquity, when the Shang arose they had Yi Yin in the Hsia (Xia). When the Chou (Zhou) arose, they had Lü Ya in the Shang. Thus enlightened rulers and sagacious generals who are able to get intelligent spies invariably attain great achievements. This is the essence of the military, what the Three Armies rely on to move.

o   o   o

The *Art of War* strikingly concludes its discussion of warfare with an infamous chapter on covert agents. The earliest known treatise on clandestine intelligence gathering, "Employing Spies" was subsequently much vilified for its purported unrighteousness and inhumanity. However, in Sun-tzu's mind nothing could be more inhuman than waging war without adequate information about the enemy and their intentions, thereby exposing the troops to needless hardship, incurring excessive casualties, and dangerously prolonging campaigns at enormous risk to the state. Because the open-source information that can be acquired by diplomats, traders, and other observers is limited and possibly erroneous, covert intelligence is vital to thwarting enemy plans and balking alliances, to achieving victory without combat.

As exemplified by Lü Ya, a defector rather than a clandestine agent, and Yi Yin, a Shang agent who gathered vital information from the king's disaffected consort, by Sun-tzu's era spies had already enjoyed a long lineage, having thus been employed during the earliest dynastic revolutions. They assumed many forms and undertook a myriad missions; indeed, beautiful women were even employed for their ability to distract and debauch as much as to ferret out information. (The PRC and North Korea still maintain specially trained contingents of women dedicated to executing such missions.)

Subsequent to the *Art of War*, as documented in our *Tao of Spycraft*, clandestine practices proliferated and increased attention was devoted to the theory and practice of spycraft. Coordinated assaults and systematic programs that included bribery, assassination, and estrangement techniques contrived to buttress the state's martial power and directly subvert others. (All these practices continue as integral parts of contemporary PRC doctrine, just as clandestine information gathering marks many Asian countries and commercial enterprises.)

Although their origins remain important and often underlie the very possibility of success, the five types of spies are defined by their functions. Local spies or "village guides" being crucial for invading forces, they would usually be drawn from residents and prisoners. For preparatory work and ongoing intelligence gathering, however, the other categories were primary, the most productive being government members (ranging from high-ranking officials to lowly doormen) and double agents.

In contrast to "expendable" agents, whose fate is hopeless, "living spies" come closest to the contemporary concept of a covert agent. Because disinformation agents are normally terminated when the deceit is discovered, ruthlessness is required in their employment, their deliberate sacrifice being justified by larger humanitarian concerns. The spymaster must be characterized by wisdom, perspicacity, and resoluteness to undertake such enormous responsibilities.

Afterword

Doctrine and Implications

Despite the enigmatic character of the text, a fundamental vision pervades the entire *Art of War*. Because warfare is the greatest affair of state, every effort must be devoted to what might succinctly be termed "the ruthless practice of efficient warfare." Although a dark realization, it should not be confused with the perversity of recent forays into cataclysmic conflict or the deliberate ruthlessness identified with thirteenth-century Mongol onslaughts that sought to overawe potential resisters by systematically slaughtering entire cities. Instead, the *Art of War* unfolds an all-encompassing conceptual and operational vision that emphasizes a thoroughly analytical, conservative approach to preserving life and property to the fullest extent possible while not wasting efforts to prevail.

However isolated and disjointed, the loosely thematic chapters and numerous specific pronouncements may all be seen as expressions of this overriding martial intent. Several core concepts provide the theoretical foundation for the book's strategic analysis, operational principles, and detailed tactics, all of which entail often unseen interconnections and implications. Despite impressions to the contrary, no outright contradictions plague the text, the few noticeable inconsistencies being resolved within the broader concepts.

Insofar as the theory and practice of warfare is thought to have extended applicability beyond the martial realm, once the *Art of War*'s fundamental vision has been exposed and its essential orientation grasped, the core concepts, the major operational principles, and the tactical measures can be adopted into various spheres of human endeavor, especially those characterized by competition or outright conflict, however circumscribed and muted. Although somewhat delimited by their internal dynamics and martial origins and therefore not entirely plastic, the potential applications are virtually unlimited, constrained only by the reader's perspective and imagination. Employing the strategies in this fashion falls into the fundamental and traditional Chinese orientation toward knowledge-based, inventive strategies and tactics that allow even disadvantaged, outnumbered forces to prevail.

Not surprisingly, in the Later Han the *Art of War* was classified under the subcategory of *ping ch'üan mou* (*bing quan mou*). Although roughly translatable as "military power and planning," *ping ch'üan mou* can also be understood as "strategies for achieving a military imbalance" because *ch'üan* (*quan*) is generally identified with expediency, with military measures that stress volatile tactics, swiftness, and indirection to achieve their aims. "Experts in *ch'üan* and *mou* preserve the state with the orthodox and employ the army with the unorthodox. Only after first estimating the prospects for victory do they engage in warfare. They unite the disposition of troops and strategic power, embrace *yin* and *yang,* and utilize technology and crafts." Many of the numerous clever techniques and stratagems formulated in its wake over the centuries, such as those found in the infamous *Thirty-six Stratagems* and visible in the thick compendiums widely available today, derive their impetus from the *Art of War*.

Fundamentals

Once warfare forcefully displaced ritual observances and became acknowledged as the greatest affair of state, its undertaking and practice demanded the utmost effort in every dimension. Rational planning and objective assessment became the basis; and, according to Sun-tzu, gaining one's objectives, whether political or military, without engaging in conflict, became the highest ideal. Coercion soon constituted a legitimate military instrument, but frustrating the enemy by balking their plans proved particularly satisfying. Accomplishing these aims necessitated the sort of detailed intelligence that could be gathered only through active effort and the aggressive use of clandestine agents. Thereafter, whether in the diplomatic arena or on the battlefield, the enemy could be compelled and enervated, manipulated and weakened, until the imposition of overwhelming strategic power easily vanquished them.

Although Sun-tzu advocated the deliberate calculation of the probable outcome before engaging in combat, he was also cognizant of the inescapable nature of external threats and the possible need to defend oneself through expeditionary strikes and even preemptive actions. Competition and conflict being inherent to virtually every structured human endeavor, strife often proves inescapable even in the personal sphere. Nevertheless, the most extemporaneous responses must be not only rationally conceived but also fully and resolutely exploited, never marked by quivering or hesitation to preclude reverting to a position of likely defeat. States may have the leisure to plod through and weigh possible courses of action, but individuals trapped in the immediacy of ordinary life usually do not.

Within the purview of armed conflict, the fundamental principle of organizational unity must first be realized. All the members of the basic entity must be fully in accord on the group's values and intentions. For a dedicated effort to be sustained under the stress of battle, they must embrace the avowed objectives and enthusiastically support the core "vision." Strategic plans and prolonged conflicts, the latter eschewed for being fraught with danger and likely to debilitate the state, therefore require consensus building and complete allegiance to the leadership. Absent any of these, failure is inevitable and doom likely.

Problems invariably arise because the world frequently proves neither logical nor predictable. Events stimulate greed, nurture anger, and provoke a desire for revenge, all of which adversely affect rational assessment and the ability to formulate optimal coping strategies. Accordingly, although acknowledging that anger provides the battlefield impulse necessary to slay the enemy, the *Art of War* strongly warns against becoming emotionally embroiled in conflicts.

Even if the requisite conditions for engaging in warfare can be achieved, prolonged conflict must still be avoided because it debilitates the participants, causes generalized unrest, and destabilizes the government to the point of making it vulnerable to internal rebellion and external assault. It is not just shooting wars that exhaust the participants but interminable strife in every realm. Building an unassailable position to reduce vulnerability and deter attacks thus ranks as a paramount measure. Therefore, contrary to ideas voiced by proponents of relying solely upon virtue and righteousness, cultivating formidable strength and thereby overawing potential enemies may prove the most efficient course of all.

Even if commanders have a dedicated commitment to the *Art of War*'s principles, strategic and tactical planning remains impossible without a thorough knowledge of the enemy and yourself. Sun-tzu's famous assertion that "one who knows the enemy and knows himself will not be endangered in a hundred engagements" should not be trivialized despite its frequent citation. Major expeditionary campaigns and other actions of commensurate importance in more personal and commercial realms always require extensive planning based upon thorough knowledge of not just the opponent's capabilities, desires, and intentions but also one's own.

Detailed calculations were traditionally performed before mobilizing for a campaign, more specific assessments presumably being made by the field commander before engaging the enemy. Despite being undertaken in the ancestral temple, the calculations were not a form of divination but were probably based upon systematically assigning estimated numerical values to various criteria and factors, such as those identified in "Initial Estimations." The importance of further detail and of apparently minor but pivotal issues may be seen from the forty or so the book notes in total. Some, such as Heaven and Earth, are defined as interrelated pairs, others simply as values and their absence or contrary, including prosperity, unity, effective rulership, social order, economic and military strength, discipline, vigilance, and various indicators of competence in command. Similarly, the comparative state of readiness or vulnerability might be assessed by analyzing such pairs as hunger and satiety; exhaustion and rest; order and disorder; fear and confidence; cold and warmth; wetness and dryness; and laxity versus alertness.

These concrete benchmarks are less important than identifying and enumerating a set of applicable, realistically assessable criteria and transforming the effort into an art or science rather than making it a mere exercise in enthusiasm. It would hardly seem necessary to us to reiterate this concept given the emphasis upon planning, economics, and numbers in business today. Nevertheless, a close examination of recent corporate debacles reveals that plans and projects are often predetermined, that they are based upon someone's whim, vision, or instinct—not necessarily an inimical practice because inspiration must originate somewhere—subsequent efforts and data all being directed to supporting the new orientation or objectives.

Nations have similarly and inappropriately embarked on war and taken other actions, covert or manifest, armed with faulty data, and many apparently ill-fated military actions have stemmed from defective or inadequate intelligence. Sun-tzu's confidence that sufficient concerted effort would always succeed in determining the underlying reality accounts for his stress on the aggressive use of intelligence agents. But although the structured semifeudal world was marked by complexity and intrigue, the tempo of events was often ponderous and the battlefield possibilities far more circumscribed.

Generals and Authority

Although less applicable for any but the most complex business organizations, the question of ultimate and derived authority looms large within the context of warmaking. The defining incident of Sun-tzu's legendary career—the probably apocryphal demonstration with the palace women—reflects the ever increasing complexity of the era's strife and the accompanying shift from warrior-led contingents to professionally commanded armies. (Similarly, visionary entrepreneurs and innovators often cling to ultimate power long after soaring expansion has mandated the employment of professional managers with specific expertise in marketing, management, and finance.) Not surprisingly, as rulers became estranged from the realities of combat, clashes inevitably arose between the civilian authorities and those entrusted with military power.

Vested interests and power groups such as the literati who were becoming the government's professional administrators apart, there was a well-recognized and fundamental clash between the values, practices, discipline, and temperament appropriate to the two spheres. The impossibility of communicating also posed an insurmountable obstacle: The court was incapable of reacting to campaign issues or battlefield developments given that the most cryptic information would require hours to relay by signal fires, days or weeks by other methods. Accordingly, Sun-tzu felt compelled to condemn interference in the commander's field authority.

As the recent conflict between the secretary of defense and the U.S. military over the nature, components, and direction of the 2003 Iraq invasion has illustrated, this is hardly an antique issue. The struggle between civil and martial authorities over who will plan, control, and exercise the ultimate power entrusted to the military heatedly continues despite general recognition (at least in the United States and most European countries) of the priority and necessary dominance of the former. Not simply a matter of political versus military authority, it impinges upon and suffuses all aspects of a civilization in its determining of cultural priorities, values, and goals.

Furthermore, continuing unabated is the generalized shift from diffused responsibility that entrusts localized combat leaders with executing the commander's intent to the micromanagement of the digitized battlefield by increasingly higher-level authorities, computerized systems, and even distant civilian authorities ensconced in various bureaus and agencies. (Similar issues apply in large organizations, corporations, and conglomerates as exact practices rather than general methods and measures are rigidly specified.) Thus, although political issues define the objective and determine the state's recourse to war, civilian authorities in recent decades have increasingly insisted upon setting the permissible operational parameters and specifying strategies, deployments, force levels, and even individual targets, thereby obviating professional experience and knowledge as well as endangering the army.

Insofar as field commanders control the fate of their men and indirectly that of the state, Sun-tzu identified a broad range of essential characteristics that must be sought. Although combat clearly demands the greatest courage, that quality alone was deemed neither adequate nor primary, wisdom being accorded that role, as might be expected given the *Art of War*'s heavily rational approach to warfare. Yet no single virtue, no matter how extremized, would be sufficient; whereas numerous faults (such as a commitment to fame or reputation) were viewed as easily prompting hasty, ill-conceived, or erroneous actions that result in defeat.

"Initial Estimations" defines the commander's requisite characteristics as wisdom, credibility, benevolence, courage, and strictness, but many more are scattered throughout the text. When compiled, these characteristics provide a profile for all leaders, civil or military, corporate or organizational, the assumption being that they are to be sought complete when appointments are made. Outstanding commanders are marked by wisdom, knowledge, credibility, strictness, benevolence, courage, tranquility, analytical skill, disdain for fame and punishment, devotion, obscurity (in plans and actions), uprightness, strength, self-discipline, cleverness, and inventiveness. Conversely, the flawed or benighted commander is unenlightened, brutal, fearful, lax, overly solicitous, cowardly, incapable of fathoming the enemy, vain, obsessed with fame, easily angered, hasty to act, weak, and arrogant.

An immediate consequence of articulating and recognizing sets of desirable and inimical traits is their focal manipulation. Although, as extensively outlined in our *Tao of Spycraft*, later texts would discuss how even the greatest virtues might systematically be turned to advantage, Sun-tzu has already suggested measures for exploiting certain character flaws, such as perturbing commanders if they are angry and deferring to them to foster arrogance. Similar principles apply to all realms of human conflict and endeavor, the most forceful necessarily being reserved for the direst of situations.

The Psychology of *Ch'i*

Fundamental to many aspects of Chinese thought ranging from metaphysics to medicine, protoscience through religion from at least the Warring States period

on, *ch'i (qi)* is essentially the *pneuma,* or vital energy of
life. Because *ch'i* is a metaphysically tinged pseudotech-
nical concept, popular tradition tends to imagize it as
originally derived from nurturing vapors rising from a
cauldron of steaming rice. At birth, humans receive an
original *ch'i* component that provides the very foundation for courage, but its level or activity fluctuates
according to time and circumstances. Because it is somewhat malleable, it is assumed to be capable of deliberate
cultivation and focused expression, of being directed
and controlled by will or intention. Being a crucial battlefield element manifest in the form of the army's fervor, courage, and commitment, it is therefore viewed as
an object for manipulation. Commanders strive to stimulate and nurture it in their men, enemies to repress
and enervate it.

Because it is essentially synonymous with the enemy's will to resist, to endure hardship and deprivation,
on a larger scale *ch'i* constitutes a key objective in contemporary warfare conceptions. Writ small, whether on
an isolated portion of the battlefield or in ordinary human endeavors, it is visible in the energy committed to
a task and its sustainability. Material conditions and the
prolonged stress of combat or work tend to deplete resolve and weaken effort; undermining the spirit and adversely affecting individual and collective performance
are doubts about the objective, the competence of commanders, the reliability of equipment, the current tac-

tics, the operational procedures, and even bad luck and omens. Usually the most difficult tasks are those of motivating the members of forces unified by common interests and goals, if not fate itself, and sustaining that motivation.

Cognizant of these issues, the astute commander employs his troops in constrained fashion unless and until a greater and overwhelming effort is required. Even though modern battle is premised upon unremitting onslaughts that overwhelm the enemy by applying concentrated strategic power, interfering with their decision and reaction cycles, and shattering their will to resist, it has proved difficult for expeditionary armies to maintain a highly zealous tempo much beyond forty-eight hours or a sustained one, as in World War II, past several weeks.

Corporate and other civil life situations must be even more restrained, but in all circumstances Sun-tzu recognized the possibility of suddenly eliciting maximum effort for a limited period by throwing the troops onto "fatal terrain," whether physical or merely situational and thus figurative. Correspondingly, although confined configurations and other naturally occurring obstacles should always be turned to advantage, the enemy must not be inadvertently compelled to mount a last-ditch defense or berserk counterattack. Acumen, skill, and finesse are all required because advantages and killing grounds must still be fully exploited.

Deception

Sun-tzu's identification of "deception" as the essence of warfare has proven not only one of the most intriguing aspects of the *Art of War* but also the cause of its vilification by hypocritical moralists of every guise in traditional China and the West. But Sun-tzu advocated deception explicitly in just two brief statements: "Warfare is the Tao of deception" and "The army is established by deceit." Nevertheless, in our age with its insistence upon oversimplifying, the book's many teachings have often been reduced solely to one: "Be deceptive."

However clever and enticing, and despite being the very foundation of the unorthodox, deceptive measures were never intended to be practiced for themselves; instead, they were to be created and used to guarantee the achievement of political and military objectives. Various "tricky" techniques at every level, strategic through tactical, including feigned alliances, peace initiatives, feints, prevarications, disinformation, expendable spies, multiple troop deployments, false surrenders, dragging brush, camouflage, and deliberate chaos are all designed to facilitate the manipulation and befuddling of the enemy, to cause confusion, inappropriate actions, and imbalances that might readily be exploited.

Despite never having been historically favored by U.S. forces and now being displaced to a certain extent by political correctness and the battlefield's growing transparency, deceptive practices paradoxically continue to multiply in contemporary life. Survival in the maelstrom of corporate conflict is routinely accomplished by cheating, misleading, and deceiving, though often without any systematic intent or dedicated objective. Although presumably problematic for organizations that theoretically bind behavior through laws and accountability, few constraints apart from good will and reputation restrain individuals. Thus, various forms of deception are regularly practiced in all spheres of human interaction, including the battle of the sexes, virtually all the time.

The Formless

Concrete dispositions and actions, all inescapably having discernible appearance, or "form," can be observed and fathomed by the enemy; yet their visibility can also be employed to deceive and manipulate. Being formless, however, is the true key to obfuscating and mystifying opponents and preventing them from anticipating plans or thwarting intentions. Sun-tzu therefore emphasized secrecy and opaqueness; indeed, he valued them more highly than mere feints or deceit because of their effectiveness in causing the doubt, consternation, and wasteful efforts that ensure the development of the gaps and voids so necessary for the easy penetration of the enemy. Nevertheless, being formless may also be attained through creative deceit and other unorthodox methods, including manifest but false forms that create a virtual cloud of obscurity by concealing the true state of affairs.

Despite the present fascination with secrecy, and despite secrets themselves multiplying by the myriad, in an age of mass media it is no longer fashionable to be formless and unfathomable. Inherently entailing unpredictability, these traits mark their practitioners as dubious, unreliable, and untrustworthy, invariably fatal flaws. Even in the military and intelligence realms, where extraordinary efforts are expected to maintain "formlessness," readily accessible, open sources routinely provide America's enemies with precise information about strengths and weaknesses, doctrine and budgets, intentions and methods. Debacles and deficiencies are blatantly discussed in various service journals as well as online; and in the electronic media, pundits of every type, ranging from insightful, experienced experts to virtual fools, outline, analyze, and predict every combat commitment and military mission.

Businesses fare little better because image building, maintaining an aura of energy, and stimulating enthusiasm in the high-velocity world of marketing often require that plans and products be unveiled at their incipient stage, well before they have been fully formulated and realistically evaluated, an obvious formula for failure. Minimal thought is given to depriving opponents of vital information by implementing surprising, effective programs. Ironically, transparency at too early a stage may, as it can for an army that is being exposed in the field throughout the day, result in enervation or a general loss of interest, as well as facilitate rapid encroachment and upstaging by competitors.

Configuration of Terrain

The impact of terrain is generally neglected by highly mechanized, contemporary armies except in extreme environments, but the *Art of War* commences by noting the importance of terrain and the concept of configuration occupies a significant portion of three other chapters. The recognition of recurring, describable topographical features, a crucial element in traditional Chinese military science, certainly predates the *Art of War*, astute commanders long having been wary of confined areas, wetlands, and other difficult terrain, as well as having exploited them whenever possible. In addition, prompted by radical differences in temperature, rainfall, peoples, minerals, plants, character, behavior, customs, and language, by the early Warring States the concept of regional characteristics had similarly become well established.

Without doubt, the *Art of War* initiated the systematic identification of terrain configurations and the correlation of tactical possibilities, thereby developing a body of operational principles that cohered with the fundamental assumptions of the newly evolving, infantry-based maneuver warfare. Although it can reasonably be assumed that whoever "gains the advantages of Heaven and Earth" will prevail, it is not simply because of the inherent advantages but because analysis and measurement will allow their exploitation. Everything depends upon terrain because "terrain gives birth to measurement" and leads in turn to determining requisite force levels and their deployment, as well as other measures that shape the battle space.

Realizing and exploiting the advantages of terrain generally ensure that the army's power, however limited, will be effectively applied; the result will be the overwhelming effect imagized as a great surge of water carrying all before it. Accordingly, the enemy's forces should be compelled to move through difficult areas that will enervate and dispirit them; they should be manipulated or enticed into entering easily targeted, deadly ground; and they should be vanquished when confined, enervated, and immobile. Collateral techniques to buttress the effect and to structure the enemy's movements, including disinformation, facades, and artificial obstacles, should all be employed in a dedicated, well-directed effort. The few may then readily

attack the many, achieving success that initially sur-
prises onlookers but seems easy in execution.

At first glance, the topic would seem to have few implications for contemporary, nonmilitary readers, but it
does foster a greater consciousness of the environmental
effects (expressed in part by Heaven's role), irrespective
of activities or projects. Moreover, "configuration of terrain" can also be taken figuratively, employed to catego-
rize or describe work and personal situations, whether
conflict-oriented or not. However, the key then becomes actively structuring the environment, shaping
the personal (or perhaps marketing) battle space so that
it is conducive to ambitions and intentions while being
inimical to naysayers and opponents. Simply positioning yourself and relying upon the flux magically to
produce victory, as some contemporary interpreters en-
vision, would be a delusion.

Strategic Power and Timing

Sun-tzu's analogies of a log perched atop a hill or of
a reservoir of water cascading down a mountain—techniques employed throughout China's lengthy military
history, as our *Fire and Water* extensively discusses—
provide remarkably dramatic, lucid images of latent
power and its effects. Later commentators, deeply im-
pressed by the powerful aquatic effects of typhoons and
seasonal flooding, particularly emphasize the image of

collected water suddenly unleashed in a continuous display of enormous impact. Thus, when properly configured and realized, strategic power will not only devastate enemies but may even deter them from mounting assaults or overawe them into fleeing or submitting. In addition, troops finding themselves amidst such power will naturally be caught up in its fervor and so become lethal warriors who confidently plunge into battle and easily annihilate reluctant opponents.

The temporal nature of the strategic configuration of power is often overlooked. Military might, no matter how great, when improperly applied as the result of a timing error not only wastes resources but also betrays plans and intentions. Thus the *Art of War* states: "The strategic configuration of power of those that excel in warfare is sharply focused, their constraints are precise. Their strategic configuration of power is like a fully drawn crossbow, their constraints like the release of the trigger." As the analogy requires, the application must be instantaneous, not gradual or diffused.

Even in the civil realm, whether in business activities or in resolving hierarchically structured or personal problems, premature or unfocused efforts frequently lead to failure, to dissipating energy and impact. Although the subject of innumerable books and articles in recent decades, the idea of the "proper moment" for new products, corporate strategies, military actions, or individual exertions remains easy to discuss but nearly impossible to determine. Despite the most extensive planning, careful situational analysis, and enthusiasm in execution, many fail miserably yet may prove highly effective at a different time. This unexpected success may stem from a change in environment (Heaven) or terrain (Earth), but generally results from coherence with the flux or exigencies of the moment.

A close reading of the *Art of War* suggests that rather than being passive or trusting to luck, the proper moment should be created by alertly manipulating the enemy and structuring the battle space. Thorough preparation, such as positioning logs along the side of a mountain or collecting water in a temporary reservoir, then ensures flexibility in controlling the moment of release. Thereafter, tenaciousness and the exploitation of hard-won advantages are required in the swirl of extemporaneous developments.

The Unorthodox and Orthodox

The critical concept of the unorthodox appears in just one succinct passage found in "Strategic Military Power," where it is coupled and contrasted with the "orthodox" and prioritized as the "unorthodox and orthodox" rather than "orthodox and unorthodox." At about this time, as reflected in the *Tao Te Ching*'s assertion "With the orthodox govern the state, with the unorthodox employ the army," there was already a tendency to conceive of military efforts as distinctly unorthodox in contrast to the regular, upright, virtuous, and orthodox administrative measures of civil government. In Sun-tzu's conception, the unorthodox not only is crucial for achieving victory but is the very crux of the military, the key to resolving stalemates, extricating oneself from disadvantageous situations, and overcoming superior enemies.

Puzzled by the apparently nebulous nature of the unorthodox, over the centuries numerous commentators have ventured off into hopelessly esoteric and mystical contemplations, yet commanders have also oversimplified it to introducing an element of surprise or to employing uniquely designated unorthodox forces, primarily cavalry. In anchoring Sun-tzu's approach to battle, the concept, although not completely amorphous, has virtually unlimited application. Similar possibilities apply to ordinary life situations as well. Unorthodox measures may be formulated at every level ranging from the political and grand strategic down through campaign, operational, and finally tactical levels. It is at the tactical level, however, that most leaders historically exploited the elements of surprise by being unexpected and acting in a manner contrary to that of normal procedure; in this way, they could quickly overwhelm their astonished enemies.

Although the theory and practice of unorthodox warfare over the centuries requires a book in itself (such as our *Unorthodox Warfare: The Chinese Experience*), as already noted, "orthodox" tactics obey the basic rules that govern general situations and employ troops in normal, conventional, expected ways while stressing order and deliberate movement. In contrast, "unorthodox" tactics are primarily realized through employing flexible forces in imaginative, unconventional, and unexpected ways, deliberately (but not simply or naively) acting in ways contrary to normal expectation and thereby incorporating a major element of surprise. Therefore, instead of mounting direct chariot attacks, unorthodox tactics rely on circular or flanking thrusts; instead of massive frontal assaults, they follow indirect routes to stage sudden, behind-the-lines forays.

What might be termed "unorthodox" always depends upon two factors: well-known, time-honored practice and the enemy's projections. The definition thus inescapably depends upon current anticipation within a particular battlefield context, as well as the commander's style, imagination, repertoire of tactical techniques, and tolerance for risk. Thus, an inventive commander who frequently exploits unusual techniques—such as Han Hsin (Han Xin) did in lashing large ceramic jars together so that he could ferry his troops across the river well above the enemy before mounting a surprise attack—will naturally be expected to resort to unorthodox tactics. Conversely, in situations clearly meriting unorthodox measures, a simple frontal assault may easily penetrate the enemy because the latter's forces have been diffused to preclude flank assaults and unexpected feints, thereby creating gaps and fissures just as Sun-tzu advocated.

The concept lends itself to extreme complexity and although often misunderstood or dismissed as simplistic, it remains a descriptive tool for tactical conceptualization, for characterizing and manipulating forces within an enemy's matrix of expectations more than some sort of transformational mode to be actualized in the concrete reality of men and weapons. Nothing is mysterious or mystical about the unorthodox and orthodox and their mutually productive relationship, yet later commentators and strategists, when not disdaining the practice of unorthodox techniques (to their later regret) often became seriously confused, thereby turning a useful tactical conceptualization into an unnecessary obstacle to clear strategic thinking.

The unorthodox's applicability in broader life contexts, although somewhat constrained by legality and convention, is nearly unlimited. Unorthodox approaches to problem resolution and strategy formulation stress imagination, "thinking outside the box," the art of being unexpected, and the ability to analyze situations from unconventional perspectives. More successful in marketing and corporate practice, unorthodox actions still provide the possibility of escaping or resolving personal crises, street confrontations, and even marriage difficulties, at least according to contemporary Hong Kong seers. An orientation to the unorthodox also provides the possibility of variety, just as it facilitates the commander's avoidance of repeating previous tactics, however successful, and thereby becoming predictable.

Particularly important, the unorthodox has long been viewed as providing the disadvantaged—whether outnumbered, weak, lacking connections, or inexperienced—with the means for envisioning alternative approaches and converting initially hopeless situations to advantage. Deception as to intent and execution is an integral element; tricks and facades, duplicity, battlefield dummies, feigned retreats, and even false surrenders all facilitate its use. Accordingly, coupled with various hard weapons and other concepts, such as the assassin's mace—a weapon of last resort—it continues to be a core concept in contemporary PRC military doctrine.

Final Contemplations and Pernicious Implications

As the impact of Sun-tzu's thought continues to expand, it seems appropriate to conclude by contemplating a few complex, basically pernicious issues raised by the *Art of War*. The most common nonmilitary adaptation has undoubtedly been in the business realm where

Western interpreters not only have been lecturing and writing for some decades but also have composed various dedicated tomes, including three-hundred-page, highly systematic volumes replete with modern case studies and justifications.

It is always puzzling to see sophisticated audiences of experienced executives sit in rapt attention as self-styled experts pontificate upon practices supposedly derived from Sun-tzu, yet they are so fundamental that without them no company could ever survive. Except perhaps for those self-motivated entrepreneurs (especially in China) who simply plunge into commercial activities, the book's significance and utility lie in stimulating the consciousness of various critical issues, providing a new perspective or mode of thinking, and suggesting unorthodox approaches and varied insights rather than providing basic business education.

Whether pondered for life or for commercial applications, certain fundamental aspects should not be overlooked. First, in seeking to subjugate or physically destroy the enemy, warfare's objectives definitively differ from noncombative aims. Although executives are sometimes murdered in certain countries and many CEOs would gladly see their competitors driven out of business, in civilized cultures it is the corporate entity that is targeted for extinction, not the lives of its members despite the sometimes severe economic adversity they suffer.

Second, the *Art of War* was intended for independent, semifeudal rulers and thus premised upon relatively powerful geopolitical states that could effectively mobilize their populace and diverse material resources. Although major corporations and transnational conglomerates often seem to be similarly unlimited, smaller firms and individuals, being highly constrained in both respects, have far different energy dynamics.

Third, "warfare" is necessarily unremitting and interminable in business and in life, whereas apart from exceptional circumstances—such as the extended conflicts of World War II or Vietnam—states are infrequently involved in shooting engagements that voraciously consume men and materials, even though they continuously operate in hostile political environments. In contrast, individuals and businesses are inescapably immersed in a quest for survival characterized by constant low-level strife occasionally punctuated by moments of intense emotional, fiscal, or other conflict.

The *Art of War*'s emphasis upon acquiring and analyzing all available information for the purpose of formulating an effective plan and decisively dispatching the enemy has been particularly championed. Although contemporary corporate culture thoroughly understands the need for intelligence, it is surprising that competitors and even the marketplace are infrequently studied in a truly focal way. Instead, an ever shifting variety of assumptions underlie marketing decisions, great confidence being placed on marketing surveys. Focus groups, with their inherent deficiencies, are often allowed to dictate product features. In the United States, competitive products are rarely analyzed in the sort of detail undertaken by most foreign corporations; companies as a result forfeit real information that could provide a basis for planning or action.

Aggressive intelligence gathering and balking (or subverting) the enemy's plans are of course fraught with complex legal and ethical overtones. Although Western business writers usually gloss over or simply ignore the *Art of War*'s darker mandates and implications, *within the context of war* Sun-tzu clearly called for covert intelligence gathering and the employment of every means to manipulate, compel, and subvert the enemy. Over the years, East Asian books and articles on adopting Sun-tzu have stressed the acquisition of information through covert methods. Insofar as such practices allow technological leapfrogging at minimal cost and without benefit to the innovators who have invested immense resources in their perfection, they can increasingly be expected to proliferate in the military and commercial spheres.

Whether fortuitously or balefully, intelligence acquisition in our open, information-based age has been not only simplified but also greatly facilitated by miniaturization, central data storage, and other rapid technological advances. If the Minox camera and Xerox machine (as the Soviet embassy in Washington, D.C., discovered to their chagrin) posed substantial problems in decades just past, the computer, wireless networks, the Internet, and even camera-equipped cell phones now cause security nightmares. Popular media reports and discussions raise critical issues to consciousness, dedicated journals and specialized industry publications reveal immense volumes of data in precise detail, including information about the U.S. military budget and vulnerabilities in battlefield practice.

The five clandestine agents described in the *Art of War*'s "Employing Spies" have expanded over the centuries to encompass a few new operational types, many relying upon women, and numerous minor variations. Practices frequently witnessed in the commercial realm include buying information through temporary consulting contracts; bribing officials; cultivating low-ranking and often disaffected employees such as secretaries and support personnel who paradoxically have broad access to sensitive materials; and even planting listening devices. Unguarded discussions in innocuous places (such as restaurants and first-class airline cabins) have frequently been recorded, whether by competitors or by opportunistic gathers who then market the information.

Businessmen traveling in Asia are routinely seduced by attractive companions who not only wheedle information during innocuous conversations but also photograph notes and documents once they have access to

hotel rooms. Foreign countries, whether strategic enemies or close allies, are similarly known to devote extensive resources not just to political and military
information gathering but also to acquiring industrial
and commercial knowledge for subsequent dissemina-
tion to the private sector.

Whether out of moral compunction, fear of discovery,
or lack of capability and imagination, most corporations
do not actively strive to debilitate their opponents, and
they even eschew the use of measures that reasonably
fall within the somewhat elastic limits of the law. The
frequently cited admonition to compel the enemy by
"seizing something that they love" obviously provides an
impetus and basis for coercion and extortion. Actions
taken in this vein may include the legitimate hiring
away of key personnel for their expertise and competence, thereby gaining proprietary knowledge while
simultaneously destabilizing competitors and reducing
their efficiency; covertly preempting key sources for raw
materials, essential components, and offshore manu-
facturing space, or otherwise thwarting access to them
through false orders and cartel arrangements; astutely
entangling them through third parties in specious nego-
tiations that will collaterally reveal company strategy
and other essential information, including process and
product specifications; and viciously employing women,
drugs, and material inducements to smear and discredit

high-ranking corporate personnel or convert them to covert agents.

As an example of these methods in application, the impact of a competitor's forthcoming product can be undercut by leaking news or promise of similar developments; having ostensible experts question the item's advantages or reliability, suggesting that it hasn't been perfected, properly debugged, or is dangerous and likely to have a negative effect on consumers or the environment; or raising doubts about its uniqueness and features. Even more negative and perverse measures designed to thwart marketing momentum would be broad-based disparagement and disinformation campaigns that target the corporation and their products (just as they are frequently employed against individuals and their ideas). Anonymously mounted, they would employ rumor, innuendo, online accusations, and even much publicized bogus threats of bringing lawsuits for negligence in design, production, or testing because of injuries or fatalities.

When permits or regulatory approval are required in countries such as China, issuing authorities can often be induced to procrastinate or even deny them altogether. False charges of tax evasion and other forms of criminal activity can be submitted anonymously, resulting in entanglement with investigatory personnel, wasted time, major expenses, and, finally, suspicion and tarnished reputations. In many countries, strong-arm tactics and union issues can be exploited; obstructing overseas shipping and physically diverting goods is also common. Unfortunately, although it might be hoped that these and other inimical practices such as deception and sabotage would be eschewed, not only do they continue to multiply but, because they are based upon the *Art of War*, they are advocated as integral elements of contemporary business practices and must be assiduously guarded against.

This onslaught of perversity has made it increasingly difficult for states, corporations, and especially individuals to follow Sun-tzu's advice to "first be unconquerable." Gaps, vulnerabilities, and fissures will always remain even though, figuratively speaking, high ramparts and thick fortifications have been erected. Because it is nearly impossible to anticipate new covert assaults, frustrating enemy activity similarly requires imaginative measures and unorthodox techniques. For example, market share might perhaps be defended through deterrence, the latter synonymous with surpassing product quality, market penetration, ancillary support, realistic pricing, patent design, or copyright protection.

Although this formidable aggregate may dissuade many potential competitors, especially those lacking "deep pockets," from even entering the fray, niche or guerrilla marketers (as well as imitators and counterfeiters) will always pose a threat. The larger the corporation or state, the more vulnerable they become to insurgents and irregulars, including shelf companies and unscrupulous importers. Selecting and exploiting inimical terrain or deliberately focusing on difficult markets may be sufficient to cause disinterest, but may also require reassessing objectives and standards by which success will be judged. Here the image of the recluse in the mountains looms large. Presumably successful on his own terms, he remains widely deprecated by the world.

Subsequent Developments
and Further Exploration

Readers interested in learning more about Sun-tzu's era and teachings will find that our single-volume *Art of War*, which features a translation that more closely follows the original word order, includes a lengthy discussion of the historical context, an analysis of key battles, an explication of his concepts and principles, numerous textual notes, and a variety of jottings on other military matters.

However important these concepts and tactical principles, the *Art of War* did not irrevocably define Chinese military doctrine. Rather, it initiated a vibrant and continuous written tradition of military science that, although based upon and always acknowledging the *Art of War*'s contributions, explicated, transformed, and even contradicted many of its fundamental teachings. Five of the other six works attributed to the Warring States period—the *Ssu-ma Fa (Sima Fa)*, *Wu-tzu (Wuzi)*, *T'ai Kung Liu-t'ao (Tai Gong Liutao* or *Six Secret Teachings)*, *Wei Liao-tzu (Wei Liaozi)*, and *Huang-shih Kung San-lüeh (Huangshi Gong Sanlüe* or *Three Strategies of Huang-shih Kung)*—also substantially influenced and grounded subsequent thought, key passages similarly being quoted by later military manuals.

The sixth Warring States work, attributed to Suntzu's lineal descendant Sun Pin (Sun Bin), surprisingly disappeared by the end of the Han and was known only by name until being rediscovered some three decades ago in a Han dynasty tomb. Known as the *Sun Pin Ping-fa (Sun Pin's Art of War)*, it systematically expands, comments upon, and applies Sun-tzu's thought, reflecting advances during the Warring States in the theory and practice of warfare. Our translation, titled *Sun Pin Military Methods* to distinguish it from *Sun-tzu's Ping-fa*, another volume with extensive historical introduction, individual chapter commentaries, and voluminous endnotes, remains available from Westview Press.

Among the five Warring States writings just listed, the *T'ai Kung Liu-t'ao* is not just the most comprehensive but also reportedly the most widely studied by contemporary PRC strategists. All five, together with the *Art of War* and a pseudo T'ang dynasty manual titled *T'ang T'ai-tsung Li Wei-kung Wen-tui (Tang Taicong Li Weigong Wendui* or *Questions and Replies between T'ang T'ai-tsung and Li Wei-kung)* were gathered and compiled in the eleventh century to preserve traditional military knowledge vital to the defense of the much beset Sung, shortly thereafter coming to furnish a partial basis for the imperial examinations for military appointment. The seven have been translated in their entirety and provided with historical introductions and commentary in our *Seven Military Classics of Ancient China.*

A Sung dynasty work—the *Pai-chan Ch'i-lüeh (Bai-zhan Qilüe* or *One Hundred Unorthodox Strategies*—probably provides the most insightful yet comprehensive examination of traditional Chinese military doctrine. Composed by an unknown author, it briefly character-izes the hundred most significant principles and con-cepts before coupling them with illustrative battles selected from the previous fifteen hundred years. By pairing each of them with its diametric corollary, the book proceeds to show that applications must be con-textually based and derived, that "swiftness," for exam-ple, isn't always appropriate nor Sun-tzu's teachings immutable or infallible. No doubt again an expression of the Chinese penchant for wisdom-based techniques or stratagems, over the past decade the *Hundred Unortho-dox Strategies* has enjoyed resurgent popularity in the PRC and Taiwan, having been republished in several formats ranging from vernacular translations to comic-book versions, often under a variety of imaginative titles. (Our Westview Press translation, titled *One Hun-dred Unorthodox Strategies: Battle and Tactics of Chinese*

Warfare, features chapter-by-chapter commentary and suggestions for expanded application.)

Although both practices predate the *Art of War*, Sun-tzu's final chapters initiate explicit theorizing on the critical practices of covert intelligence gathering and incendiary warfare. Both rapidly developed in the Warring States period and became the crucial components of all subsequent military endeavors. Two of our works have therefore been dedicated to examining their intriguing theory and ingenious practices: *The Tao of Spycraft: Intelligence Theory and Practice in Traditional China* and *Fire and Water: Incendiary and Aquatic Warfare in China*.

Unfortunately, excluding a few specialized academic articles, little Chinese traditional military history has yet appeared in English, though readers can readily peruse various dramatic early episodes in Crump's translation of the *Chan-kuo Ts'e* and in either Watson's or Nienhauser's versions of the *Shih Chi*. Some volumes of the *Cambridge History of China* series, particularly those on the T'ang, Ming, and alien regimes, extensively cover military developments, as does F. W. Mote in his *Imperial China*.

Nevertheless, apart from Kierman's earlier *Chinese Ways in Warfare* and our own works, to date the only dedicated volumes on Chinese military history have been Joseph Needham's (and Robin Yates's) masterly technological tomes in the *Science and Civilisation in*

China series and David Graff's *Medieval Chinese Warfare, 300–900,* as well as an earlier compilation volume under his editorship titled *A Military History of China.* Fortunately, despite the continuing academic disparagement of military studies, a few intrepid scholars such as David Wright at the University of Calgary have chosen to specialize in historical Chinese military issues; and Bruce Brooks, indefatigable progenitor of the Warring States Project, and his wife, Taeko, continue to rewrite virtually all of early Chinese history, including the martial aspects. Although Web sites dedicated to Sun-tzu's thought and contemporary applicability continue to multiply, few have proved illuminating apart from *Sonshi.*

Finally, over the last decade, several works on recent Chinese martial history and contemporary PRC military issues such as equipment, doctrine, and personnel have appeared, including *Chinese Warfighting; The Lessons of History: The Chinese People's Liberation Army at 75; Modernizing China's Military; China's Use of Military Force; The Great Wall at Sea;* and *Moving the Enemy: Operational Art in the Chinese PLA's Huai Hai Campaign.* Mao Tse-tung's military writings have also been expanded and republished, though Sun-tzu rarely receives mention in them. In the area of strategic culture, Johnston's *Cultural Realism* examines the Ming experience and Michael Pillsbury's two compilations on doctrine and intentions—*Chinese Views of Future Warfare* and

China Debates the Future Security Environment—are particularly noteworthy. Given the worldwide interest in the traditional Chinese military writings, the popularity of multipart Chinese video depictions of Sun-tzu's and Sun Pin's lives and teachings in the PRC, Taiwan, and Hong Kong is hardly surprising.

Strategic Concepts and Tactical Principles

Chapter Index

Essential Tactical Principles

Issues and Tactics for Defensive Situations